D0201154

BELA BALASSA

ECONOMIC DEVELOPMENT
AND
INTEGRATION

CENTRO DE ESTUDIOS MONETARIOS LATINOAMERICANOS
MÉXICO   1965

First Spanish edition, 1965
First English edition, 1965

HF
1408
.B19

© Centro de Estudios Monetarios Latinoamericanos

Printed and made in Mexico
GRÁFICA PANAMERICANA, S. DE R. L.

INTRODUCTION

The *Centro de Estudios Monetarios Latinoamericanos* (CEMLA) has devoted a great deal of interest to the problems of economic integration in Latin America, even before the Latin American Free Trade Area and the Central American Common Market were established. The best proof of that interest is the fact that, during the last five years, the Institution has published a series of books on different aspects of economic integration and its relationship with economic development. Thus, in 1959, a series of lectures delivered by Dr. Sidney Dell, a U. N. official, was published under the title *Problemas de un mercado común latinoamericano*; in 1960, a book written by Victor L. Urquidi, *Trayectoria de un mercado común latinoamericano*, appeared; and in 1963-64, three volumes, *Cooperación financiera en América Latina, Coordinación monetaria regional* and *Problemas de pagos en América Latina*, were published. The last three works were based on regional meetings sponsored by CEMLA, or in which the Institution took a very active part.

In line with the same policy, the *Centro* invited in 1963, Dr. Bela Balassa, of Yale University, author of *The Theory of Economic Integration*, and an expert on theoretical aspects of economic integration and international trade, to deliver a series of lectures, at the Institution's headquarters in Mexico City, on economic integration and economic development. This volume is the outcome of those lectures and, in CEMLA's opinion, represents a very valuable contribution to the study of the basic problems confronting Latin America.

In this volume, Dr. Balassa analyses, in the first place, the adaptation of the customs union theory to the requirements of the developing countries. Then he deals with the role of exports in economic growth in

7

its historical perspective, and with the alternative strategies which are available at present to the less developed regions for their economic development. Afterwards, the book reviews the problems, to which little attention has comparatively been paid up to now, derived from the role that big scale economies can play in the process of economic integration. Finally, the volume concerns itself with some of the problems of economic policy that emerge, in the less developed countries, from the attempts to establish customs unions or similar trade arrangements. The book ends up with an essay on the relationship between dynamic external economies and the size of the market. This last study was originally published in *Revista de Ciências Econômicas*, of São Paulo, Brazil.

Bearing in mind the interest that the contents of this work may offer to the economists outside Latin America, the English version is published, with the cooperation of the Committee for Economic Development (CED), simultaneously with the Spanish edition.

CEMLA wishes to express its appreciation to Dr. Balassa for his invaluable and comprehensive contribution in preparing the manuscript.

8

PREFACE

Having long been interested in the relationship of economic integration and economic development, I accepted with great pleasure the invitation of CEMLA to lecture on this problem in Mexico City. The theory of integration and that of development have by-and-large lived an independent existence, and a synthesis of the two is of interest to the economist as well as to the policy-maker.

From the theoretical point of view, the principal question appears to be whether, and to what extent, the traditional theory of customs unions is applicable to the case of less developed areas. Further, should this theory prove to be inapplicable, the question arises, what theoretical principles can be of usefulness for indicating the possible effects of integration in these economies. At the same time, the policy-maker would like to know to what extent integration can contribute to economic development and also needs information on the problems integration may give raise to.

While one can hardly attempt to provide a definite answer to these questions in the course of a few lectures, I have used the occasion to give expression to my ideas on the subject and to indicate possibilities for further investigation: theoretical as well as empirical. It is my hope that the lectures may be of interest to those concerned with problems of economic integration and development, and may stimulate further research.

I wish to thank CEMLA for their invitation to deliver these lectures, and especially Javier Márquez, Fernando Rivera and Miguel Wionczek for their kind hospitality. I have made but few changes in the text of the lectures for publication, although I have updated some of the empirical material which was gathered when I was consultant to the UN Economic Commission for Asia and the Far

East. Finally, I wish to thank Richard D. Irwin, Inc. for permission to use material from my two books, *The Theory of Economic Integration* and *Trade Prospects for Developing Countries*.

BELA BALASSA,
Associate Professor of Economics
Yale University.

10

CHAPTER I

INTEGRATION OF DEVELOPING COUNTRIES AND CUSTOMS UNION THEORY

ECONOMIC DEVELOPMENT AND INTEGRATION

Economic development and economic integration have only recently assumed prominence in public discussions. Colonialism and nationalism had their sway until World War II, and efforts to contribute to the development of colonial territories, or to remove tariff barriers between independent national economies, had little success. Neither did the countries of Latin America —that had been politically independent for over a century— make much progress on the road toward economic development.

Yet, although under different names, development and integration had their day in popular thinking and in the economic literature of earlier periods. After Britain had emerged as the major industrial power, other nations bent on industrialization attempted to find ways to reach the same status. Given the technological and financial advantages of the British, politicians as well as economists deemed to establish the necessity of raising tariff-walls to protect fledgling industries of little competitive power. The McKinley tariff in the United States, the Méline tariff in France, and tariff protection under Bismarck in Germany represented the consolidation of protectionist tendencies in these countries, and the culmination of efforts by would-be industrialists and influential writers such as Carey in the United States and Friedrich List in Germany.

13

As regards economic integration we can refer to the Zollverein, whose history provides evidence of the inter-dependence of economic and political issues, and to the formation of national economies in the seventeenth and eighteenth centuries throughout Europe. Tolls and taxes on commodities, and restrictions on the movement of labor and capital, limited economic intercourse among the small principalities, the territories subjected to a Comte or Graf, and the independent cities, so that in-tegration —the removal of discriminatory barriers— became a precondition for the formation of national economies.

It is of interest to indicate at this point the similarities between the national integration of the past and the international integration of the present. Both faced the problem of enlarging the market, allowing for the free movement of goods and productive factors, and establishing the "rules of the game" —the ways and means of policing economic activity. The differences are quantitative rather than qualitative. The removal of barriers within a national economy, the abolition of the taxing authority of a Duke or a Landgraf, and the free-dom of workers to migrate from country to town had been a great accomplishment in the time of Colbert and Friedrich the Great. But improvements in transpor-tation facilities and the concomitant reduction in the cost of transportation have since widened the potential market for individual enterprises, and technological progress has also had the effect of increasing the size of industrial establishments. In addition, with the great-er complexity of the industrial structure, external econo-mies have assumed importance, so that, while Belgium might have been considered a national economy of "ef-ficient size" a century ago, she now judges it advanta-geous to become part of a larger unit.

I have noted that development and integration became matters of public concern following the Second World War. The reasons for the emergence of these issues are not difficult to discern. As regards economic development, it was felt that political independence in the former colonial territories had to be accompanied by independence in economic relations; at the same time, in countries that had been independent before, the experience of the great depression with falling sales and prices of primary products gave rise to demands for a more diversified economic structure. In turn, political rather than economic considerations created the basis for integration efforts in Western Europe, although the economic aspects of integration soon came to the fore.

The emergence of development and integration as policy objectives has been accompanied by an intensive discussion of these problems in the economic literature. We find a certain degree of interdependence here: the raising of the questions being followed by academic discussions, and the examination of the issues by the economist bearing influence on the decision-making process. Rosenstein-Rodan's famous article on "The Problems of Industrialization of Eastern and South-Eastern Europe" came at a time when economic development had not yet become a public issue, for example, while Viner's study on customs unions was undertaken in response to the integration movement in Western Europe. Also, the spate of books written on development and integration over the past decade has been no doubt motivated by the important place these problems have come to occupy in public discussions as well as by the desire to contribute to a new branch of the economic discipline. Development economics has been created, and the theory of integration has come to lead an in-

15

dependent existence within the study of international economics.

I have mentioned economic development and integration together, but this should not lead you to believe that these two issues have come to live a joint existence. The contrary would be nearer to the truth. The theoretical literature of economic integration dealt almost exclusively with customs unions of industrial economies; in turn, in writings on economic development, the existence of national frontiers was taken as a datum and little attention was paid to the possible consequences of a fusion of national markets.

The separation of the issues of integration and development was not limited to the theoretical literature, however. Whereas integration in Western Europe was designed to remove barriers among national economies, development was conceived as the sheltering of the economies of individual nations from world competition and the loosening of ties with the world market. The paradox becomes even greater if we consider that while in Western Europe industrial economies of substantial size joined forces in order to reap the alleged benefits of a wide market, in underdeveloped regions larger units were broken up to create independent states whose economic viability is open to question.

Tribal enmities often account for the break-up of larger units inherited from colonial times, as in the case of Burundi and Rwanda; political differences appear to have motivated the separation of Senegal and Mali, while disparities in resource endowments are said to be responsible for the fiasco of the West Indian union. And one may add personal ambition for acquiring and retaining power which has strongly influenced the history of the Central American republics and has also played a role in modern Africa.

As a result, independent national states have been

16

created —some with a population of less than one million— that are smaller in size than an average French department. Examples are the former French Congo, Gabon, Mauritania and Sierra Leone in Africa, while in the Americas the ranks of independent states with a population of less than 2 million (Costa Rica, Honduras, Nicaragua, and Panama) have been joined by Jamaica, Trinidad, and British Guiana. Each of these states bears the burden of a governmental administration, declares itself in need of foreign aid, and makes an effort to develop economically.

The decline of intra-regional trade in Latin America and in Asia is a further manifestation of the process of disintegration observed in the less developed areas. According to UN statistics, in the ten-year period up to 1961, intra-Latin American trade declined by 15 per cent, while imports into the region rose in approximately the same proportion. And although in the case of Asia one should take account of the decline in entrepôt transactions, this cannot fully explain the fall in intra-area trade from $2.9 billion to $2.1 billion that accompanied the increase of extra-area imports by one-half during this period. The relative, if not the absolute, share of intraregional trade declined in Africa and in the Middle East, too.

At the same time, the emergence of interest in economic integration in the less developed countries appears to have been motivated more by the desire to imitate the European example and to escape the discriminatory effects of the European Common Market than by the objective of fostering economic development through integration. Latin American countries became increasingly concerned with the possibility of losing their European market outlets in tropical and temperate zone foodstuffs, and many expressed the opinion that the establishment of a strong regional organization was necessary to counter the discriminatory effects of the European Common Market. As late as in 1961, the President of Uruguay stated in his opening address to a conference of Latin American countries that "the formation of a European Common Market and EFTA constitutes a state of near-war against Latin American exports. Therefore, we must reply to one integration with another; to one increase of acquisitive power by internal enrichment by another; to inter-European cooperation by inter-Latin American cooperation".[1]

Among developing regions, integration was first considered in its relationship with economic development in Latin America, but integration has only recently become an *idée force* —although not a reality— in Africa and in Asia. It is interesting to note that, again, countries at a higher stage of development began to ponder the need for integration while poorer economies lagged behind. And the average size of countries in Africa —however it is measured— is considerably smaller than in Latin America.

Changes in the economic literature have been even slower. The separation of development economics and the theory of economic integration has persisted and only recently have efforts been made to link them up in a meaningful way. In this connection, the first question to be answered is to what extent the traditional theory of customs unions can be useful in examining the problems of economic integration in less developed areas.

THEORY OF CUSTOMS UNIONS: TRADE CREATION AND TRADE DIVERSION

The expression, "the traditional theory of customs

[1] Cited in Sidney Dell, *Trade Blocs and Common Markets*, London, Constable, 1963, p. 161.

unions" is used here to refer to a series of writings from Viner to Lipsey that dealt with the question as to how the desirability of customs unions can be determined. Following Viner, the test has been whether a customs union is, on balance, trade creating or trade diverting. Trade creation refers to the increase of trade among the member countries of a customs union, and trade diversion to the reduction of trade with the outside world, both following the removal of internal trade barriers in a union.

If countries A and B form a union, new trade will be created, inasmuch as the removal of intra-union tariffs will make possible the exploitation of differences in production costs that was prevented beforehand by reason of the existence of duties. After integration, resources will be reallocated and each country will expand the production of commodities it can manufacture at lower costs.

On the other hand, the non-participating country C will be discriminated against in an integrated area; whereas, before the formation of the union, the producers of country C faced the same tariff barrier in country B as did $A's$ producers, after integration the former will have to scale the common tariff of the union while the latter pays no duty. Under the assumption of constant costs, if country C supplied A with the commodity in question prior to integration but the sum of $C's$ production costs and the common tariff of the customs union exceeds the cost of production in member country B, the latter will supplant C as a supplier of the commodity in question to country A.

Trade creation and trade diversion are basically welfare concepts that are designed to indicate the impact of the formation of a customs union on the allocation of economic resources within the union and in third countries. This conclusion is further strengthened if consideration is given to the refinements of the Vinerian concepts of trade creation and trade diversion by making allowance for inter-country differences in production costs and the so-called consumption effects.

If account is taken of differences in unit costs, welfare gains and losses derived from the establishment of a union are represented by cost-savings or increases in costs rather than by the amount of trade created or diverted. The welfare gain will therefore refer to savings in costs resulting from the shift of purchases from higher cost to lower cost sources of supply within the union, while the welfare loss relates to the extra costs of producing a commodity in the partner country rather than in the foreign country. Instead of trade creation and trade diversion, we may now speak about the positive and negative production effects of integration.

A further distinction is made between production effects and consumption effects. Whereas production effects result from shifting purchases of a given commodity from more expensive domestic to cheaper member country sources of supply (positive effect), and from lower cost foreign to higher cost member country producers (negative effect), consumption effects entail the substitution of commodities produced in partner countries for domestic goods and foreign goods. Consumption effects can also lead to an improvement or a deterioration in welfare. Whereas the abolition of discrimination between domestic goods and the commodities of partner countries represents an improvement (positive consumption effects), the newly created discrimination between the commodities of partner countries and the products of foreign countries on the market of the home country (negative consumption effects) will reduce welfare.

I have elsewhere indicated the similarity in the logic applied to production effects and consumption effects. While production effects tend to be favorable if increased purchases of a given commodity from a member country take place at the expense of domestic rather than foreign sources of supply, positive consumption effects will predominate if consumers substitute the commodities of partner countries for domestic goods rather than for foreign products. The analogy can be pursued further if we regard commodities as different ways of "producing" utility. For example, the consumer can choose between domestic and imported wine or between home produced wine and imported whiskey. Now the choice between sources of supply of wine (production effects) finds its parallel in the choice between sources of utility derived from the consumption of wine or whiskey (consumption effects).[2]

Thus, the traditional theory of customs unions deals with welfare gains and losses that are associated with the reallocation of resources following the establishment of a union. This statement should be qualified to refer to a *given* amount of resources that are reallocated after the union is formed. In addition to the reallocation of existing resources, welfare gains and losses can also be derived from (2) economies of scale; (3) changes in the terms of trade; (4) forced changes in efficiency due to increased foreign competition; and (5) a change in the rate of economic growth. But, as Lipsey notes, "the theory of customs unions has been almost completely confined to an investigation of (1) above, with some slight attention to (2) and (3), (5) not being dealt with at all, while (4) is ruled out of traditional theory on the assumption (often contradicted by the facts) that production is carried out by processes which are technically efficient".[3]

[2] Bela Balassa, *The Theory of Economic Integration*, Homewood, Ill., Richard D. Irwin, and London, Allen & Unwin, 1961, p. 59.
[3] R. G. Lipsey, "The Theory of Customs Unions: A General Survey", *The Economic Journal*, September 1960, p. 496.

The question arises as to what extent the traditional theory of customs unions can be applied to less developed countries. To answer this question we should first consider the various factors that are said to determine the trade creating or trade diverting effects of a customs union. These are: the complementarity or competitiveness of the participating economies, the size of the integrated area, propinquity and transportation costs within the union, the degree of economic intercourse among the participanting countries prior to integration, and the height of tariffs before and after the union's establishment.

COMPLEMENTARITY AND COMPETITIVENESS

To begin with, the definition of the concepts of complementarity and competitiveness should be recalled. According to Viner, competitiveness (rivalry) can be characterized as "correspondence in kind of products of the range of high-cost industries between the different parts of the customs union which were protected by tariffs in both of the member countries before customs union was established".[4] Thus competitiveness means a considerable degree of overlapping in the range of protected commodities produced in the countries that participate in the customs union. Since production in the member countries had taken place behind protective tariff walls before the union was established, gains can be obtained by removing tariffs and thereby achieving a more efficient resource allocation among the countries in question. The gains will be the larger, the greater are the differences in production costs.

On the other hand, if the member countries of the union are complementary, i. e., they are producing a

[4] Jacob Viner, *The Customs Union Issue*. New York, Carnegie Endowment for International Peace, 1950, p. 51.

different range of commodities, we can expect that trade diversion will be strong. This conclusion follows since, after the removal of tariff barriers among the member countries, imports will be obtained from a higher cost member country instead of a lower cost nonparticipating country. Complementarity will not give rise to trade diversion, however, if the union includes the lowest cost producer.

The concepts of competitiveness and complementarity appear to be useful in judging the possibilities of trade creation and trade diversion in a union of developed economies, such as the European Common Market or the European Free Trade Association. Aside from agriculture, the Common Market economies are largely competitive, for example, but the countries participating in the European Free Trade Association are to a considerable extent complementary; whereas Britain is a large exporter of manufactured goods, several of the other member countries rely on the exports of raw materials and semi-finished products.

Concerning the possible usefulness of these concepts in judging the desirability of a union of developing countries, it should be recalled that the exports of developing countries consist chiefly of primary commodities, while manufactured goods weigh heavily in their imports. For purposes of the present discussion, four groups of commodities may be distinguished. Among primary products, I will separately consider commodities that are produced *and* exported by a large number of developing countries, and goods that are produced only in a few of these countries and are traded within the less developed regions. As regards manufactured goods, distinction will be made between nondurable consumer goods that are presently produced in many of the developing countries and durable manufactures that are largely imported from industrial areas.

The first group of primary products includes a number

of tropical commodities, such as oilseeds, cocoa, coffee, tea, cotton, and bananas. Oilseeds are produced and exported in various African and Asian countries, for example; bananas are exported by all countries of Central America, while coffee is produced by Brazil and several other countries in Latin America, as well as by a number of countries in Africa. Aside from the case when price supports are applied in the countries in question, we cannot expect a reallocation of resources to take place after integration, since these countries are competing on the world market and will continue to do so after the union will have been established. And even in cases when price supports are applied in some of the countries under consideration, the reallocation of resources will be restricted as long as the countries participating in the union maintain their national identity. This conclusion follows given the fact that, in the face of uncertainties relating to the future demand and price of primary products, countries strive for a certain degree of diversification in their exports.

Take the case of Brazil, for example. Brazil used to rely almost exclusively on the exportation of coffee but has recently expanded her exports of cotton, meat, and several other products. Although Brazil may have comparative advantage in coffee over other Latin American producers, one could hardly compel Brazil to become again a one-crop economy —especially if we consider that Brazil would not be immune from competition on the part of African producers.

Turning to primary products that are produced in one or two countries of a region, and are imported by others, we find that the outcome will depend on availabilities as well as on economic policies followed in the individual countries. In the case of fuel and nonfuel minerals and some tropical products (e. g., hard fibers), differences in climate and resource endowments account for the existence of trade, and hence the elimination of tariff barriers can hardly create new trade. On the other hand, in the case of primary commodities whose domestic production is protected by various forms of trade restrictions (cotton in Argentina and wheat in Brazil are examples), the removal of protective barriers would lead to an expansion of trade.

A third group of commodities includes various manufactured products designed primarily for consumption, such as textiles, shoes, cigarettes, and some food products. These commodities are presently produced by a large number of less developed countries, chiefly in Latin America and in Asia, and production often takes place behind high tariff barriers. Given differences in production costs, a reduction in trade barriers would create new trade and thereby lead to a reallocation of resources.

I come now to the fourth group of commodities which are not presently produced in less developed areas or are produced only in a few countries. This group of commodities includes chemicals, machinery and transport equipment as well as durable consumer goods. Since the majority of these commodities are not produced in developing countries, we can hardly speak about trade creation or trade diversion in a static context. Rather, the consideration of prospective trade in these products should be postponed until a later lecture.

One may conclude that the categories of competitiveness and complementarity have only limited usefulness in judging the desirability of a union of developing countries. While the Vinerian definition of competitiveness as an overlapping in the range of *protected* commodities is applicable to the case of various nondurable consumer goods and some temperate zone foods, it has little relevance to the bulk of the commodities exported by these countries. Further, the concepts of comple-

25

mentarity and competitiveness will not find application to intermediate products and capital goods that account for one half to two-thirds of imports into less developed countries, since only a few of these commodities are presently produced in less developed areas.

The Size of the Union

The next question concerns the size of the economic area encompassed by a union. It has often been argued that the larger the economic area of the union, the greater is the potential scope for the international division of labor, and therefore the larger will be the benefits of a customs union. While a smaller customs union may lead to useful shifts in some lines of production, the chances for the reallocation of production are said to increase with the expansion of the area; also, successive increases in the size of the union are assumed to reduce the possibility of trade diversion.

In attempting to apply these propositions to a union of developing countries, we face the problem as to how the size of a national economy or a customs union can be measured. Various definitions of market size have been suggested. Some have argued that the size of a union should be measured by population or by the geographical area. Such a concept would not indicate the possibilities for specialization in an integrated area, however, and it would lead to the misleading conclusion that, e. g., the economic area of China or India was greater than that of the United States.

A more appropriate measure would be the volume of production, or, rather, the gross national product exclusive of the contribution of the subsistence sector. But, in judging the effective size of an area, account should also be taken of differences in tastes and the costs of transportation. For a given marketable output, the greater is the cost of transportation and the more diversified

26

the tastes of the population, the smaller will be the effective size of the market.

The effects of transportation costs on intra-regional trade will be discussed at a later point, thus I will presently limit the discussion to a few remarks concerning tastes and consumption patterns. Among less developed countries, differences in tastes are perhaps the least important in Latin America, but are of considerable significance in Asia and in Africa. The tastes and consumption pattern of the Central African Negro are different from those of the North African Arab, for example, and differences are found also in the consumption habits of the inhabitants of, e. g., Thailand and Afghanistan. But while differences in tastes are of importance at the present time, the integration of these countries is bound to lead to changes in consumption patterns and, in the process of economic development, tastes are likely to become more uniform, making thereby possible the standardization of a variety of consumer goods. Thus, the consideration of existing differences in tastes will have only limited relevance in judging the desirability of customs unions in less developed areas.

Should we disregard the qualifications relating to differences in tastes and transportation costs for the time being, a comparison of the gross national products of various areas will be of interest. It should be noted at this point that national income estimates for the developing countries involve a considerable degree of error and, at the same time, differences in the pattern of consumption between developed and underdeveloped countries reduce the value of international comparisons. Still, the data provide an indication of relative magnitudes.

According to calculations made by Rosenstein-Rodan,[5]

[5] P. N. Rosenstein-Rodan, "International Aid for Underdeveloped Countries", *The Review of Economics and Statistics*, May 1961, p. 118.

the gross national product of the Latin American republics amounted to about 18 per cent of the U. S. gross national product in 1951, while the corresponding ratio was 14 per cent for the countries participating in the Latin American Free Trade Association, and one-half of one per cent for the Central American Common Market. At the same time, the combined gross national product of the former British West Indies has not exceeded one-third of one per cent of the gross national product of the United States. Turning to other continents, we find that the GNP of the less developed countries of Asia amounts to about one-fourth of the U. S. GNP, while this ratio is only 1 per cent for Malaysia, 8 per cent for Africa, and 3 per cent for the Middle East.

These comparisons would point to comparatively small gains obtainable through the reallocation of resources in a union of developing countries, especially if account is taken of the fact that a considerable portion of the GNP of these countries is produced in the subsistence sector. But the static character of the comparisons should not be forgotten. The smallness of the national markets of less developed economies is, in part, due to the low level of economic development in these countries, so that economic integration *cum* development will enlarge their markets. Correspondingly, a comparison of the present size of national or regional markets will have only limited usefulness for indicating the possible gains derived from integration in less developed areas.

Further, whereas under static assumptions a comparison of the market size of customs unions may provide an indication of the benefits of integration, in absolute terms, more interest attaches to the relative gains that individual countries would obtain from joining the union. In general, one would expect that, for a union of a given size, the greater is the increase in the size of the market for the producers of individual countries, the larger will be the gains from integration. Thus, a union of ten small countries would bring greater gains than the integration of two large national economies.

I have noted before the existence of a large number of small countries in underdeveloped areas, especially in Africa. It may then be argued that these countries could obtain considerable gains from the reallocation of resources in the framework of an integrated area, and the economic benefits of joining a free trade area or customs union would be greater for Nicaragua than for Brazil, and for Gabon as compared to Egypt. Yet, although this proposition is applicable under static assumptions, here again dynamic considerations are likely to be decisive, and, in the case of substantial intra-regional disparities in levels of development, a large and relatively developed country may in fact gain more than a small and backward economy.

Our discussion would not be complete without mention being made of the possibility that the establishment of a customs union could result in changes in commercial policies. Those who contend that there is a positive correlation between the size of the union and the gains derived from the reallocation of resources have explicitly or implicitly assumed that the union's creation will not lead to changes in commercial policies; on the other hand, it has often been argued that the larger is the union, the greater will be its bargaining power and the more it will be inclined towards protectionism.

There can be little doubt that concerning this last proposition, integration increases the combined bargaining power of the participating countries, and hence a union is often able to get better terms, at tariff negotiations. The reaction of the European Common Market to the raising of tariffs on carpets and glass by the United States is a case in point. The increase of these tariffs had an adverse effect chiefly on Belgian exports and it appears questionable whether Belgium, or, for that matter, the Benelux union, would have retaliated against the United States. The Common Market, however, immediately retaliated by raising duties on U. S. exports of comparable magnitude.

The assertion that protectionist tendencies would necessarily prevail in an integrated area is open to question, however. Similar allegations had been made over a decade ago in regard to the European Payments Union, yet, despite the pessimistic forecasts the EPU has not become a sheltered, high-cost area. Some may also be inclined to dispute the proposition that protectionist tendencies tend to predominate in the European Common Market. But, how about Latin America or Asia? Would regional economic unions in these areas not have a protectionist character?

The answer is in the affirmative if comparison is made with a hypothetical free trade situation. However, if we consider that the countries in question engage in protection behind national tariff-walls, the degree and the cost of protection may well diminish as the narrow national markets are superseded by a large, integrated area. At the same time, the problem of protection in less developed areas cannot be considered solely in terms of welfare gains and losses in a static context, without paying attention to its implications for economic development. Therefore, we may usefully postpone the discussion of this question until a later lecture.

TRANSPORTATION COSTS

I have already referred to the fact that transportation costs reduce the effective size of a market area. In this connection, note should be taken of the primitive state of the transportation network —especially surface trans-

portation— in less developed regions. Given the poor facilities for land transport and inland waterways, about
nine-tenth, of existing trade within Latin America and
within Africa uses the sea route, for example. But the
use of ocean transportation, too, is often hampered
by the inadequacy of land and water approaches that
link the ports with their hinterlands, the insufficiency
of harbour facilities, and the lack of regular shipping
lines. Correspondingly, the cost of transportation between Latin American ports and New York, and between
African ports and London is in many cases substantially
lower than between ports on the same continent.

A consideration of transportation costs would, then,
speak against the establishment of a union including
all countries of Latin America or all countries of Africa.
In turn, some argue that, as trade begins, the need for
improved transportation becomes pressing, and appropriate facilities will, in some way or other, be subsequently established. In other words, the expansion of
trade would lead to an imbalance between trade and
transportation facilities, and this imbalance would bring
forth the desired response.

Both of these propositions are open to objections,
however. One can hardly take the present state of transportation facilities as given without considering the possibilities for future improvements, for example, since
following the same line of reasoning the "integration"
of the United States could also have been objected to a
little over a hundred years ago.

Thus, although the construction of transportation facilities has an opportunity cost in the form of alternative
investments foregone, the lack of overhead capital in
the form of transportation equipment should not be used
as an argument against the integration of all of Latin
America or all of Africa.

At the same time, the relationship between trade and

transportation is by no means simple. They might reinforce each other to develop a "virtuous circle" of increasing trade and improving transportation facilities as it happened around the turn of the century in Mexico, or a "vicious circle" as shown by the experience of some regions in Argentina. To start a "virtuous circle", appropriate arrangements have to be made for improving transportation facilities, unifying transport regulations, and equalizing transport costs.

TRADE AMONG PROSPECTIVE MEMBER-COUNTRIES

It has further been argued that the possibilities of specialization can be indicated by the degree of economic intercourse among the prospective union members. According to this proposition, the existence of intensive trade-relations among the prospective member countries will indicate the possibilities of further specialization. This proposition has again proved to be useful in evaluating the desirability of customs unions of developed countries. It has been pointed out, for example, that the low proportion of trade conducted among the countries participating in the European Free Trade Association, as compared to trade among the member-countries of the Common Market, indicates less favorable prospects for trade creation and a high probability for trade diversion. But, is this proposition applicable to a union of developing countries? Before answering this question, we should look at the relevant figures.

Whereas before the establishment of the European Common Market, 36 per cent of the foreign trade of the participating countries was with each other, the corresponding proportions are 22 per cent for Asia, 13 per cent for the Middle East, 7 per cent for Latin America, and 7 per cent for Africa. Therefore, with the exception of Asia, the degree of economic intercourse among countries that would participate in a regional union is rather small. Asia is a special case, in part because of the importance of entrepôt trade. Further, India and Hong Kong export considerable amounts of cotton textiles to countries of Southeast Asia, while India imports large quantities of foodstuffs from the area. On the other hand, manufactured goods account for only a small proportion of intra-regional trade in Latin America, the Middle East, and Africa.

But the low degree of economic intercourse in underdeveloped areas should not be used as an argument against their economic integration, since differences observed in regard to intra-area trade in Western Europe and in underdeveloped regions reflect, to a large extent, disparities in the level of their economic development. While far reaching specialization has evolved among the highly industrialized economies of Western Europe, the exchange of commodities is limited in low income areas that specialize in primary products.

Several further factors that have hindered the expansion of intra-area trade in underdeveloped regions should also be mentioned. I have referred before to the inadequacy of transportation facilities in underdeveloped regions, the adverse effects of which are augmented by the virtual absence of market information and distribution channels. Import quotas and multiple exchange rates have had similar effects, since in general the lowest priorities had been assigned to commodities produced domestically (or desired to be produced domestically), and thus consumer goods manufactured on a small scale in some of these countries have rarely become objects of exchange. Further, political and economic ties with the former colonial powers impeded economic intercourse among African countries, while in Latin America the system of bilateral trade and payment agreements discriminated against intra-regional trade.

33

The removal of discriminatory restrictions can thus create possibilities for the expansion of intra-area trade. Still, the main question is not how much trade will increase after these restrictions are removed, but rather the extent to which economic development in an integrated area contributes to intra-regional exchange. This consideration lies outside the scope of the traditional theory of customs unions, however.

TARIFF LEVELS

Our last point refers to the height of tariffs. It can be easily seen that, *ceteris paribus*, the higher the average level of initial tariff on trade among the participating countries, the greater will be the expansion of trade due to the elimination of duties. At the same time, trade diversion will be greater, the higher are the duties levied on products originating in third countries.

Given the high tariff levels in the countries of Latin America, these propositions would indicate the possibility of a considerable degree of trade creation *and* trade diversion in this area. But an appropriate discussion of this question again requires a consideration of the effects of tariffs on economic development. At the same time, in other less developed regions quotas are more important forms of restrictions than tariffs and hence the height of tariffs will not appropriately indicate the protective effects of trade restrictions.

CUSTOMS UNION THEORY AND INTEGRATION IN LESS DEVELOPED AREAS

In today's lecture I have inquired into the applicability of the traditional theory of customs unions to economic integration in less developed areas. We may now conclude that the factors which are said to determine the trade-creating and the trade-diverting effects of a customs union have only limited relevance for a union of developing countries, since they do not allow for the interrelationship of economic integration and development. By considering the reallocation of existing resources and taking universal free trade based on static comparative advantage as its welfare criterion, the traditional theory of customs unions will thus be of little usefulness for evaluating the desirability and the possible consequences of integration in less developed areas. The question arises, then, what theoretical considerations will be relevant for our purpose. This will be the subject of the following lectures.

CHAPTER II

EXPORTS AND ECONOMIC GROWTH

EXPORT-ORIENTED GROWTH AND THE INDUSTRIAL REVOLUTION

In the first lecture, I indicated the emergence of interest in problems of economic development and integration since the Second World War and examined the applicability of the traditional theory of customs unions to economic integration in less developed areas. The conclusion has been that, by reason of its static assumptions, the traditional theory has only limited relevance for a union of developing economies, and hence it is necessary to explore what theoretical principles can find application in evaluating the probable effects of integration in less developed areas.

I wish now to suggest that the issue of integration should be considered in the general context of the study of economic growth. In this connection, I will raise several questions. Among these I include the role of trade in the process of economic growth during the nineteenth century, the changing structure of international trade in the present-day world, and the possibilities of economic growth based on the production of primary commodities. As regards the latter, I will present some results of projections which I have prepared regarding the future prospects for the exports of developing countries.

In surveying the writings of economic historians, one finds considerable emphasis on problems of supply, together with a virtual neglect of considerations of demand. While much space has been devoted in the literature to capital accumulation, the increase of the labor force, the emergence of the entrepreneurial class, and related questions, little attention has been paid to the role of markets in the process of economic growth. It seems as if economic historians had been under the spell of *la loi des débouches* and had implicitly assumed that whatever is produced can be sold. Although three decades ago E. W. Gilboy exhorted historians to pay more attention to demand factors,[1] until quite recently her plea met with little response, and it remained for Goran Ohlin to point out that "the first step towards an understanding of the growth process is simply to pay as much attention to the growth of an industry's market as is usually lavished on the growth of its capacity".[2]

This criticism does not apply to German historians, however, among whom Werner Sombart deserves special mention for his insistence on the importance of demand-induced growth. In his *Luxus und Kapitalismus*, Sombart inquires into the origin of several consumer-goods industries, and finds that the expansion of textile production, the production of leather goods, etc., owes much to the demands upon them in royal and baronial courts. The availability of funds for purposes of luxury consumption thereby provided an incentive for improvements in the processes of production and for the use of new materials and fabrics. At the same time, so Sombart argues, the wars of the sixteenth and seventeenth century greatly contributed to the development of heavy industry. In his *Krieg und Kapitalismus*, he notes that

[1] E. W. Gilboy, "Demand as a Factor in the Industrial Revolution", *Facts and Factors in Economic History*. Cambridge, Mass., Harvard University Press, 1932, pp. 620-39.
[2] Goran Ohlin, "Balanced Economic Growth in History", *American Economic Review, Papers and Proceedings*, May, 1959, p. 353.

the demand for more sophisticated and effective weaponry led to improvements in the steelmaking process and to the more intensive use of nonferrous metals, and it also played a role in the emergence of a rudimentary machinery industry.

But economic historians should not shoulder all the blame. Keynes expressed the view that, since the time of Ricardo and Say, much of the economic theory had been based on the implicit acceptance of the proposition that supply creates its own demand. This statement —meant to apply to the theory of income determination— has special relevance to discussions of economic growth. Growth models are generally supply-oriented with virtually no account taken of demand factors.

At the same time, considerations of economic growth found little place in the theory of international trade during the first half of this century. Trade theorists were generally preoccupied with the question of the reallocation of resources through trade and, despite occasional references to the importance of trade in economic growth, problems related to the development of economic resources fell outside the field of inquiry.

The static orientation of international trade theory was not the intention of its founders, however. Adam Smith noted the interrelationships between trade, economic growth, and market size, and John Stuart Mill called attention to the impact of trade on tastes and technology. It appears that these writers saw the main benefit of international trade in its dynamic effects and —to borrow a felicitous phrase from Sir Dennis Robertson— they realized that trade can be "an engine of growth".

Thus, while Sombart emphasized the role of demand for luxury goods and military hardware in the process of industrialization, Smith and Mill laid stress on the contribution of international trade to economic growth.

This shift in emphasis might have been due to changes in the relative importance of the factors contributing to industrial development; the factors mentioned by Sombart assisting in earlier periods, and international trade assuming importance at a later stage.

EXPORTS AND ECONOMIC GROWTH IN BRITAIN

The role played by foreign trade during the Industrial Revolution in Britain should first be noted. A small island with limited natural resources, the growth of the British economy would have been retarded, had England not been able to find outlets for her industrial products and exchange them for primary commodities. According to a recent interpretation offered by K. Berrill "the most vital circumstance for the first industrial revolution was the market condition in the trading area, and this was slowly ripening before 1780".[3] This interpretation has also been endorsed by H. J. Habakkuk and Phyllis Deane who have argued that the "take-off" of the British economy had originated in a sudden acceleration of exports.

Export-oriented development characterized the leading sector of the British economy of that time, the textile industry. Within a few decades, the production of textiles had grown from small-scale establishments serving exclusively the home market into a large industry, 60 per cent of whose products were for exports.[4] The breakthrough in the textile industry, in turn, provided a stimulus for the iron industry via demand for steam engines and textile machinery. The availability of export markets was instrumental in the expansion of other British manufacturing industries, too, as witnessed by

[3] K. Berrill, "International Trade and the Rate of Economic Growth", *Economic History Review*, 1960 (3), p. 350.

[4] Phyllis Deane and H. J. Habakkuk, "The Take-off in Britain", *The Economics of Take-off into Sustained Growth*, ed. W. W. Rostow, London, Macmillan, 1963, p. 78.

the increasing share of exports in British national income. Even without cotton textiles and iron goods, the volume of exports increased by one-half between 1779-1793, and another one-third in the following decade. Correspondingly, the share of exports in the British national income rose from 10 per cent in 1780 to 16 per cent in 1800.[5]

After a temporary decline during the Napoleonic wars, exports further increased in importance in the second period of rapid growth of the British economy around the middle of the nineteenth century. Schlote shows that the annual rate of increase of exports was 5.3 per cent in 1840-1860, exceeding the rate of growth of national income by a considerable margin.[6] Comparisons of increases in exports and national incomes are of special importance since, as Nurkse has emphasized, for the purposes of evaluating the role of international trade in economic growth, the incremental relationship between trade and national income rather than their average ratio is relevant.

While the rapid expansion of exports had made possible a high rate of growth of incomes in Britain during the time of the Industrial Revolution and around the middle of the nineteenth century, the slackening in the rate of increase of exports contributed to a slowing-down of economic growth in subsequent decades. After 1870, the annual rate of growth of exports fell from 6 to 2 per cent in Britain; correspondingly, the share of exports in national income declined from 27 per cent in 1872 to 16 per cent in 1900 although it rose again to 22 per cent in 1913.[7]

[5] *Op. cit.*, p. 340.
[6] Werner Schlote, *British Overseas Trade*, Oxford, Oxford University Press, 1952, pp. 42, 49.
[7] C. P. Kindleberger, "Foreign Trade and Economic Growth: Lessons from Britain and France, 1850 to 1913", *Economic History Review*, 1961 (2), p. 294.

Various explanations have been offered to explain the interaction of exports and economic growth in the period of deceleration of British growth. The most ingenious and straightforward is that of Professor Kindleberger. Kindleberger notes that around 1870 the British had three-fourths of the world market in cotton textiles, iron rails, galvanized iron, tinplate, locomotives, ships, and coal, and the maintenance of past growth rates in the exportation of these commodities was not compatible with the expansion of world demand and the emergence of new competitors. Accordingly, Britain could have maintained past growth rates in exports only if she had modified her production and trade pattern.[8]

More generally, a country with a lead in industrial production can sustain past growth rates in the face of a slackening of the rate of growth of world demand or the emergence of new competitors if she can transform the structure of her economy. Instead, Britain chose to redirect her exports towards new markets in India, the Middle East, and China. The redirection of exports can, and did, at the time we are talking about, provide a short-term remedy but it could not halt the decline in the rate of expansion.

TRANSMISSION OF ECONOMIC GROWTH THROUGH INTERNATIONAL TRADE

I have indicated the role of exports in the process of economic growth in Britain during the nineteenth century. It appears that exports were a leading sector in the British economy and, in the hundred years up to 1870, the share of exports in national income tripled. At the same time, Britain's decision to forego agricultural protection, coupled with her increasing need for raw materials, contributed to an approximately parallel

[8] *Op. cit.*, pp. 295 ff.

rise in imports, so that imports also grew at a rate greatly exceeding that of national income.

Economic growth in Britain was thus transmitted to her suppliers of grain, cotton, timber, meat, and other primary commodities. This circumstance, as well as increased demand for primary products on the part of the industrializing continental countries, goes far to explain the attainment of rapid rates of growth and high living standards in several primary-producing countries in the temperate zone. Australia and New Zealand are well-known examples, while in Western Europe, Sweden and Denmark deserve mentioning.

Youngson notes that, in the second half of the nineteenth century, "the expansion of Swedish timber trade was not initiated by changes of any great importance in the conditions of supply", but rather the important changes "originated outside Sweden's borders, and were part of the early extensive industrialization of Western Europe".[9] Timber exports, directed towards the United Kingdom and continental Europe, grew at an annual rate of 6.5 per cent between 1830 and 1850, and even faster afterwards. Between 1850 and 1872 exports increased five-fold, and greatly contributed to the growth of the Swedish economy.

In the case of Denmark, the enactment of the Corn Laws was an important development. After the liberalization of trade in grains in Britain, Denmark increased her grain exports at a rapid rate, and the rise of exports, in turn, prepared the way for the growth of the economy. Denmark also provides an example of a primary-producing country that has undergone successive transformations in search of market opportunities. Whereas, around the middle of the nineteenth century, she relied chiefly on the production of cereals, in the eighteen-

[9] A. J. Youngson, *Possibilities of Economic Progress*, London, 1962, p. 162.

45

seventies and eighties Denmark faced the competition of cheap grain originating in North America and Oceania. With the demand for meat and dairy products increasing rapidly in the United Kingdom and Germany, the Danes chose to forsake the production of cereals and to engage in livestock raising and dairying. The exportation of dairy products and meat that utilized imported grains, has enabled the Danes to attain a high standard of living. Further shifts in the pattern of specialization have taken place, more recently when uncertainties concerning future market opportunities have led to the expansion of several branches of manufacturing industry such as furniture-making.

TRANSMISSION OF ECONOMIC GROWTH AND THE DEVELOPING COUNTRIES OF TODAY

Australia, New Zealand, Denmark, and Sweden are of special interest to us in the present discussion since these countries have attained prosperity through the exportation of primary products. The question arises, whether similar opportunities exist for the less developed countries of today. In this connection, the changing structure of world trade in the last decades should be noted.

I may begin by citing the views of Raul Prebisch, the former Executive Secretary of ECLA, according to whom disparities in the growth of demand and in market structures have resulted in a slow growth of export earnings in the less developed countries. Prebisch divides the world into the industrialized Centre and the primary-producer Periphery. According to him, the income elasticity of demand for primary products at the Centre being considerably smaller than the income elasticity of demand for industrial goods at the Periphery, the exports of the latter area are rising at a lower rate than its imports, while the existence of oligopolistic market structures at the Centre together with competitive markets at the Periphery result in declining terms of trade for the countries of the Periphery. The slow rate of expansion of exports and the deterioration of the terms of trade, then, restrict the ability of the Periphery to increase export earnings and this tendency is reinforced by reason of the low price-elasticity of demand for primary products.

Prebisch's arguments may be criticized on the grounds that the high rate of increase of imports of industrial goods is, in itself, the result of decisions made by the less developed countries bent on industrialization. To use Machlup's expressions, the deficit in the balance-of-payments of the developing countries is a "programming" rather than a "market" imbalance. Doubts have been raised about the alleged differential impact of market structures on prices at the Centre and the Periphery, too.

To escape these criticisms, one may reformulate Prebisch's proposition by reference to the transmission of economic growth from developed to developing countries. I have indicated in this lecture the workings of the transmission mechanism during the nineteenth century. At that time, it was generally expected that this state of affairs would continue and that, with diminishing returns in agriculture and the exhaustion of sources of raw materials in the industrialized countries, the rate of growth of the imports of primary products into the latter areas would accelerate rather than decline. Similar views have been voiced on several occasions since; a little over a decade ago, for example, the Paley Commission warned that increasing shortages would develop in raw materials.

Various influences have acted to relieve the pressure on natural resources, however. These include increased productivity in the agriculture of the industrial countries, the discovery of new mineral deposits, the introduction of synthetics and other substitute materials, and the reduction of input requirements per unit of output. According to Prebisch and some other writers, these influences, along with the low income elasticity of demand for foodstuffs and the increase in the share of services in national income in the industrial countries, have in fact made the transmission mechanism inoperative and led to a deterioration in the relative position of the primary-producing countries.

While these writers maintain that the transmission of economic growth through international trade is a thing of the past, others have found little fault with the functioning of the transmission mechanism. To evaluate these conflicting views, and to indicate the growth-potentialities of developing countries that rely on the exportation of primary products, I will now present some empirical evidence on recent developments and projections for the period 1960-1975.

TRENDS IN THE EXPORTS OF DEVELOPING COUNTRIES

Those who assert that the rise of imports into industrial areas is falling behind the growth of incomes in these countries, usually cite the experience of the nineteen-thirties and forties as evidence. In fact, in the period 1928-1955 surveyed in a GATT study, the volume of imports into industrial countries increased by only 38 per cent while their gross national product rose by 88 per cent. And although the terms of trade moved in favor of the primary-producing countries during this period, the increase in the purchasing power of their exports did not exceed 50 per cent.[10]

[10] *Trends in International Trade*, Report of a Panel of Experts, Geneva, GATT, 1958.

But these developments were greatly influenced by the depression of the thirties and the Second World War. Especially during —and immediately after— the war a variety of measures were taken in the industrial countries with the aim of reducing imports. Several of these changes were of an once-for-all character, however, and can hardly be expected to continue. This conclusion is supported by the experience of the relatively peaceful years of the last decade; to exclude the immediate post-war years and the Korean-war period, I have compared data for the years 1953-54 and 1960-61. In this period, the gross national product of the industrial countries increased by 31 per cent, the volume of their imports originating in less developed areas rose by 48 per cent, and the purchasing power of the exports of the developing countries by 33 per cent.

Incomes and imports in the industrial countries, expressed in value terms, thus increased approximately in proportion during the last decade. This result conceals, however, large differences among individual commodity groups. To examine the underlying factors that are responsible for the disparate trends experienced during this period, I have classified the main export products of the developing countries into seven groups: temperate zone foodstuffs (meat and fish, cereals, feeding-stuffs, fruits other than bananas and wine), competing tropical foods (oils and oilseeds, sugar, and tobacco), non-competing tropical foods (tropical beverages and bananas), agricultural raw materials (hides and skins, rubber, forest products, textile fibres), nonfuel minerals and metals (metal ores, concentrates, and unwrought metal), fuels, and manufactured goods.

As regards the first three groups of commodities, the low income elasticity of demand for food should first be mentioned. Statistical investigations indicate that, in the industrial countries, the income elasticity of demand for cereals and potatoes is negative, it is zero or slightly above zero in the case of fish, oils and fats, sugar, and tea, and —excepting the case of the United States— it is about 0.5-0.6 in regard to coffee, cocoa, fruits, and meat.

Despite the relatively low income elasticities of demand, the imports of non-competing tropical foods into industrial countries rose at a rate exceeding the growth of incomes during the period 1953-54 to 1960-61, however. For one thing, imports into Western Europe were boosted by increases that had taken place from the low postwar level; for another, the decline in the prices of coffee and cocoa contributed to the expansion of consumption in all industrial countries. But, given the low price elasticity of demand for tropical beverages, the fall in prices wiped out the entire gain in the volume of imports experienced between 1953-54 and 1960-61 (Table 1).

In the case of temperate zone and competing tropical products, the situation has been aggravated by reason of the protectionist policies followed in the industrial countries and the encroachment of the United States upon world markets. Among temperate zone foodstuffs, the U. S. producers have become large exporters of cereals, while protectionist policies and productivity improvements in agriculture have contributed to an increase in the degree of self-sufficiency in Western Europe. The European Common Market has become self-sufficient in wheat, pigmeat, and butter, and the United Kingdom, the erstwhile champion of free trade, has also come to supply an increasing proportion of her food consumption from domestic sources. Still, rising U. S. purchases of meat and fish have led to an increase in the imports of temperate zone foods from developing countries by one-fourth —only slightly less than the 31 per cent rise in the gross national product of the industrial countries.

50

TABLE 1

EXPORTS FROM DEVELOPING COUNTRIES TO INDUSTRIAL ECONOMIES, 1953-54 AND 1960-61

	Volume			Unit value	Value		
	1953-54 U.S. $ Mil.	Prices 1955	1960-61 Index 1953-54=100	1960-61 Index 1953-54=100	1953-54 U.S. $ Mil.	Current prices	1960-61 Index 1953-54=100
Temp. zone food	1 541	1 954	126.8	98.0	1 691	2 100	124.3
Competing tropical foods	1 899	2 056	108.3	92.9	2 013	2 026	100.6
Non-competing tropical foods	2 881	4 044	140.4	59.2	3 258	2 708	83.1
Raw materials	3 647	3 991	109.4	107.2	2 970	3 485	117.3
Nonfuel minerals and metals	2 076	2 799	134.8	98.3	1 796	2 379	132.5
Primary products, fuels excluded	12 044	14 844	123.2	87.9	11 728	12 698	108.3
Fuels	1 846	5 327	283.7	97.8	1 811	5 025	277.5
Primary products, total	13 890	20 081	144.6	90.5	13 539	17 723	130.9
Manufactured goods	447	1 109	248.1	110.7	446	1 225	274.7
Exports to industrial countries, total	14 335	21 189	147.8	91.7	13 985	18 947	135.5
Gross national product in industrial countries, U.S. $ billion	700.70	920.5	131	n.a.	n.a.	n.a.	n.a.

SOURCE: Bela Balassa, *Trade Prospects for Developing Countries*, Table 1.1.3.

Competing tropical foods are produced in tropical climate in the less developed countries and in temperate climate in industrial areas. Sugar and oils and fats are of greatest importance here. The United States has successively reduced the share of imports in her sugar consumption through the application of quotas, whereas in Western Europe tariff protection has led to the same result. At the same time, the United States has become the world's largest exporter of oilseeds, reducing thereby the share of the less developed countries in the imports of Western Europe. Correspondingly, the per capita imports of non-competing tropical foods from less developed areas into industrial countries declined in the period 1953-1961.

Agricultural raw materials enter the production of clothing, automobile tires, lumber and paper products, and a variety of industrial products of lesser importance. While the income elasticity of demand for clothing approaches unity, the demand for textile fibers is rising at a lower rate by reason of the shift towards high-quality apparel. In addition, synthetic fibers have encroached upon the market for textile fibers and by 1960 the share of natural fibers in fiber consumption declined to 74 per cent in the United States and 70 per cent in Western Europe.

Synthetics also encroached upon the market for rubber. The income elasticity of demand for rubber is about unity in the industrial countries but an increasing share of consumption has taken the form of synthetics. Whereas in 1950 synthetic rubber accounted for 4.3 per cent of U. S. and 9 per cent of European rubber consumption, by 1960 this ratio reached 69 and 38 per cent in the two areas, respectively. Correspondingly, the consumption of natural rubber fell over the last decade in the United States, and modest increases were experienced in Western Europe.

While the shift towards synthetic materials adversely affected the export earnings that developing nations derive from the sale of natural fibers and rubber, their exports of timber expanded rapidly. The countries of Western Europe have come to increasingly rely on tropical timber to satisfy their need for quality wood, and the rise in the consumption of plywood and veneer necessitated increasing imports of tropical hardwood into the United States, too. But timber still accounts for a relatively small proportion of agricultural raw materials imported from developing countries, so that per capita imports of these materials, taken together, failed to increase in the period under consideration.

Various influences bear on the imports of nonfuel minerals and metals. Although the exact magnitude of the income elasticity of demand for the products that incorporate these materials is not known, we may assume that it is around unity. But shifts have taken place in the consumption of individual metals (e. g., aluminum has been substituted for steel and copper in certain applications), and improvements in the recovery and reprocessing of metals, as well as technological innovations such as electrolytic tinplating, have contributed to a decrease in input-requirements per unit of output in some uses. On the other hand, given the limited availabilities of mineral resources in the main industrial countries, imports of most minerals increased at a higher rate than domestic consumption. Increases were especially large in imports into Western Europe, while the decline in purchases of metals for government stockpiles restricted the expansion of imports into the United States. All in all, imports of nonfuel minerals and metals into the industrial countries rose *pari passu* with the growth of their GNP.

More favorable results are indicated in the case of fuels and manufactured goods. Although the income

53

elasticity of demand for energy hardly exceeds unity in the industrial countries, as a result of the shift from coal to oil and increased reliance on foreign supplies of petroleum the import demand for fuels increased considerably faster than energy consumption or the gross national product. Increases have been shown in regard to manufactured goods imported from developing countries, too, but these imports have remained small in absolute terms.

It appears, then, that while the export earnings of the developing countries increased approximately in proportion with the growth of GNP in the industrial areas, large differences are shown as between commodity groups, indicating the existence of considerable disparities in regard to the transmission of economic growth from developed countries to developing economies. In this connection, two questions should be raised: will the relationship between imports and incomes observed in the industrial countries during the fifties continue in the future? and, what are the expectations of developing countries that specialize in a narrow range of commodities? I will attempt to provide a tentative answer to these questions in the remaining part of this lecture. Note that in the following I will speak about the exports of developing countries to developed economies when the latter include industrial areas as well as Australia, New Zealand, and South Africa.

PROJECTIONS OF THE EXPORTS OF DEVELOPING COUNTRIES

The projections have been prepared in two variants, depending on the rate of economic growth attained in the developed countries (Table 2).

According to these projections, the volume of imports into developed countries originating in less developed areas would increase at a rate slightly exceeding the

54

TABLE 2

EXPORTS FROM DEVELOPING COUNTRIES TO DEVELOPED ECONOMIES, 1960-1975

	1960	1970 I	1970 II	1975 I	1975 II
Exports to developed countries in 1960 prices, U.S. $ million	19 496	29 097	30 479	36 010	38 915
	100	149.2	156.3	184.7	199.6
Exports to developed countries in current prices, U.S. $ million	19 496	26 734	28 418	33 054	36 217
Index	100	137.1	145.8	169.5	185.8
Implicit price index of exports	100	91.9	93.4	91.7	93.1
Gross national product in developed countries, in 1955 prices, U.S. $ billion	964.0	1 439.3	1 519.5	1 739.3	1 888.2
Index	100	149.3	157.6	180.4	195.9

SOURCE: Bela Balassa, *Trade Prospects for Developing Countries*, Table 3.1.1

NOTE: Unchanged prices have been assumed.

growth of GNP in the former. The value of imports is expected to rise at a lower rate, however, by reason of the assumed decline in the prices of some primary products. Nevertheless, the fall in these prices would be confined to the 1960-1970 period, and after 1970 the increase in the value of imports, too, would exceed the rise in the GNP of the developed countries.

But these results, again, conceal substantial discrepancies in the prospects of individual commodities and commodity groups. To begin with, low income elasticities of demand and agricultural protectionism will continue to restrict the importation of temperate zone foods into Western Europe, and an increase in these imports in per capita terms is not anticipated. With rising purchases of meat and fish, U.S. imports muy double during the period under consideration, however, and increases may be even greater in Japan. Still, given the large share of Europe in the food imports of the developed countries, imports of temperate zone foods from less developed areas would hardly rise at a rate exceeding 2 per cent a year in the period 1960-1975, as compared to the projected 4 per cent annual rate of growth of their GNP. (Estimates refer to the first income variant and are shown in Table 3.)

The prospects are even less favorable in regard to competing tropical foodstuffs. While continuing increases are foreseen in imports of tobacco, in view of the low income elasticities of demand and protectionist policies followed in the United States and Western Europe, the per capita imports of sugar, oilseeds, oils and fats will hardly rise. Further, the discontinuation of the sugar premium paid by the United States to Latin American suppliers and some declines in the prices of oils and fats are likely to limit the increase in import values to about one-half of one per cent a year.

More rapid increases are anticipated in the imports

56

TABLE 3

THE COMMODITY COMPOSITION OF THE EXPORTS FROM DEVELOPING COUNTRIES TO DEVELOPED ECONOMIES

(Current Prices)

	1960	1970 I	1970 II	1975 I	1975 II
Temperate zone foods, U.S. $ million	1 993	2 330	2 457	2 713	2 924
Index	100	166.9	123.3	136.1	146.7
Competing tropical foods, U.S. $ million	2 127	2 113	2 172	2 284	2 372
Index	100	99.3	102.1	107.4	111.5
Non-competing tropical foods, U.S. $ million	3 095	3 955	4 027	4 469	4 573
Index	100	127.8	130.1	144.4	147.8
Agricultural raw materials, U.S. $ million	3 146	3 608	3 819	4 106	4 457
Index	100	114.7	121.4	130.5	141.7
Fuels, U.S. $ million	5 085	8 260	8 976	11 030	12 570
Index	100	162.4	176.5	216.9	247.2
Nonfuel minerals & metals, U.S. $ million	2 975	4 656	5 069	6 073	6 809
Index	100	156.5	170.4	204.1	288.9
Manufactured goods, U.S. $ million	1 075	1 812	1 898	2 379	2 512
Index	100	168.5	176.6	221.3	233.7
Total exports, U.S. $ million	19 496	26 734	284.8	33 054	36 217
Index	100	137.1	145.8	169.5	185.8

SOURCE: Bela Balassa, *Trade Prospects for Developing Countries*, Table 3.1.3.

of non-competing tropical foods, although the rate of growth of imports observed in the last decade is not expected to continue. Gains are foreseen in the per capita consumption of coffee, cocoa, and bananas, but not for tea and spices. For the developed countries, taken together, a 44 per cent rise in imports has been projected, corresponding to an average income elasticity of import demand of about 0.4.

With respect to agricultural raw materials, a continuation of trends observed during the fifties is foreseen leading, thereby, to an increase in the volume of imports from less developed areas by one-half. But, given the expected decline in the price of natural fibers and, more importantly, rubber, the value of imports has been projected to rise by only 30 per cent.

It can be concluded that, as a result of the low elasticity of demand for foodstuffs, the increased self-sufficiency of industrial countries in agricultural products, and the substitution of synthetics for natural materials, the expansion in the imports of commodities of agricultural origin will continue to be slow. My projections entail a 36 per cent increase in the volume, and a 31 per cent rise in the value of the imports of these commodities from less developed areas, as against an 80 per cent increase in the gross national product of the developed countries.

A different picture is shown in regard to fuel and nonfuel minerals and metals and for manufactured goods. The imports of these commodities from less developed areas are expected to more than double in the period 1960-1975, corresponding to an implicit income elasticity of import demand substantially above unity.

In the case of nonfuel minerals and metals, the limited availability of mineral resources in the industrial countries and the shift towards importation in metal form will contribute to a rise of imports from less developed

58

areas. Increases are likely to be especially large in regard to aluminum, zinc and iron ore, and the rise of imports is expected to fall behind that of the gross national product of developed countries only in the case of manganese, lead, and tin.

Increases will be even larger in the imports of fuels, although a decline in prices as compared to the 1960 level is likely to moderate the rise in import values. With the continuation of the shift from coal to oil, imports of petroleum and petroleum products are expected to increase especially in Western Europe and Japan, and at least one developing country (Algeria) will also export natural gas to Western Europe.

Changes in the imports of manufactured goods are more difficult to foresee. In projecting trade in textiles, I have assumed that the International Cotton Textiles Agreement would be continued until 1975, while available information concerning prospective trends has been utilized in regard to other manufactured products. Taken together, the imports of manufactured goods from developing countries have been estimated to increase at an annual rate of 5.5 per cent.

These results indicate that whereas the usual arguments about the unfavorable trade prospects of the developing countries apply to the exports of agricultural products, different considerations are relevant to non-agricultural exports. And if we also consider that, according to the national plans of developing countries and forecasts prepared by international organizations, the income elasticity of import demand in the less developed areas is around unity, their exports and imports could grow approximately in proportion if rates of growth of GNP were the same in all areas, developed as well as less developed. With consideration given to the increasing burden of payments on the service account, balance-of-payments equilibrium could still be ensured by some increases in foreign aid.[11]

But while balance-of-payments considerations would permit reaching equal rates of growth in developed and in less developed areas, the question arises if this should indeed be the appropriate objective. Taking account of prospective increases in population, we find that a uniform growth rate of 4 per cent would entail a 2.8 per cent rise in per capita incomes in the developed countries and 1.6 per cent in developing economies. Thus, discrepancies in living standards would increase in absolute, as well as in relative terms.

It appears, then, that the projected expansion in the exports of the less developed areas does not allow for an acceleration of their economic growth that would be necessary to reduce international disparities in living standards. By comparison, primary-producing countries could attain high rates of growth in the nineteenth century when imports into European countries increased at a rate exceeding the growth of national incomes.

Consideration should also be given to the disparate expectations of the various developing regions. Prospective changes in export earnings will depend on future trends in the exportation of individual commodities, discoveries of mineral resources, the "pull" of established markets growing at differential rates, and the impact of the European Economic Community, on the patterns of international trade. Accordingly, the largest increase in exports is foreseen in Africa, whose producers will benefit from the exportation of recently discovered petroleum and natural gas, as well as from the rapid growth of demand for minerals and metals in Western Europe,

[11] For a detailed discussion, see my *Trade Prospects for Developing Countries*, Homewood, Ill., Richard D. Irwin, 1964, ch. III-V.

TABLE 4

EXPORTS FROM DEVELOPING COUNTRIES BY REGIONS OF ORIGIN

(Current Prices)

	1960	1970 I	1970 II	1975 I	1975 II
Latin America, U. S. $ million	7 931	9 872	10 479	11 662	12 630
Index	100	124.5	132.1	147.0	159.2
Africa, U. S. $ million	4 038	6 747	7 163	9 167	9 871
Index	100	167.1	177.4	227.0	244.4
Middle East, U. S. $ million	3 097	4 638	4 972	5 655	6 594
Index	100	149.8	160.5	182.6	212.9
Asia, U. S. $ million	4 430	5 477	5 804	6 570	7 122
Index	100	123.6	131.0	148.3	160.8
Total exports, U. S. $ million	19 496	26 734	28 418	33 054	362.7
Index	100	137.1	145.8	169.5	185.8

SOURCE: Bela Balassa, *Trade Prospects for Developing Countries*, Table 3.1.4.

and the preferential effect of the European Common Market.

With increases in the share of African oil in the world market, the rise of exports will be somewhat smaller in the Middle East, while the unfavorable composition of exports will hinder the rise of exports in Latin America and Asia. The latter two regions derive three-fifths of their export earnings from the sale of agricultural commodities and their total exports are expected to rise by about one-half in the period 1960-1975, as compared to an increase of over 80 per cent in the Middle East and nearly 130 per cent in Africa (Table 4).

We can now conclude that empirical evidence does not bear out the contention of those writers who maintain that the transmission mechanism of growth through trade has ceased to operate. But the expansion of exports indicated in our projections does not allow for an acceleration of economic growth in the developing countries that would allow for reducing international disparities in living standards. The question arises, then, what alternative strategies are open to the developing countries for accelerating their rate of economic growth. I will examine this problem in the following lecture.

Chapter III

ALTERNATIVE STRATEGIES FOR ECONOMIC GROWTH

THE ROLE OF EXPORTS IN THE PROCESS OF ECONOMIC GROWTH

In the previous lecture, I examined recent changes and future prospects for the exports of the developing countries. Presently, I will consider alternative strategies for the economic growth of these countries. In this connection, a few words should first be said on the role of exports in the process of economic growth.

Exports play a double role in the growth process. On the one hand, an expansion of exports can contribute to the rise of national income through the utilization of unemployed resources, as well as through input-output relationships, changes and technological progress; on the other, increases in exports ensure balance-of-payments equilibrium in a period of economic growth.

Little needs to be said about the utilization of unemployed resources through a rise in exports, although we should note that the word unemployed is somewhat of a misnomer here, since the resources in question might have been "dormant" in the sense that in a primitive economy there had been no demand for them. Examples are rubber and copper that are produced in less developed areas almost exclusively for exportation.

The use of resources that were not utilized before may trigger off the growth process or may lead instead to the establishment of enclave industries. To obtain

65

the first result, input-output relationships and repercussions through income-changes have to come into play. The former include the familiar backward and forward linkage-effects, while the latter refer to increases in the production of consumer goods in response to a rise in demand at higher income levels.

If, for example, a country becomes an exporter of steel, this will give a boost to iron-ore and coal-mining, while the availability of cheap steel may lead to the establishment of steel-using industries. Further, should rising incomes in the export sector be retained in the domestic economy, there will be an increased demand for consumer goods which, in turn, permits the development of industries catering to consumer demand.

In general, the effects will depend on the size of the stimulus, and the relative importance of the forward and backward linkages.

The described changes are likely to be connected with improvements in technology. Adam Smith has already noted that increasing exports will contribute to improvements in "productive powers" through the application of large-scale production methods, innovations, and improved skills. An expansion of exports may lead to the use of advanced production methods that could not be utilized before by reason of the narrowness of the domestic market, and the opportunity to export can also provide incentives to innovating activity.

It appears, then, that under favorable circumstances an expansion of exports may contribute to economic growth. At the same time, increases in exports will ensure balance-of-payments equilibrium by paying for imports that are necessary for a growing economy. The two effects do not necessarily coincide, however; export-induced growth may be accompanied by a deficit in the balance-of-payments and balance-of-payments equilibrium may be associated with slow growth or stagnation.

We may now formulate the "objective function" of a less developed economy as the maximization of the rate of growth accompanied by the maintenance of acceptable levels of balance-of-payments deficit. According to this formulation, economic growth is the main policy objective while permissible levels of balance-of-payments deficit appear as a constraint to the growth process.

A comparison of this objective function and that implicit in the traditional theory of customs unions is now in order. As I noted in the first lecture, the latter takes the efficient allocation of existing resources as its objective which, in turn, is said to be served by universal free trade. Correspondingly, the traditional theory judges the desirability of customs unions according to their trade creating and trade diverting effects, and the establishment of a union of developing countries would be considered undesirable if it were, on balance, trade diverting.

But trade diversion may be called for if export possibilities are limited. It has been argued, for example, that an increase in the export supply of primary products from developing countries, in excess of the rise of demand on the part of developed countries, would be accompanied by a fall in export prices, and, assuming the price elasticity of demand for primary products to be less than unity, export earnings would decline rather than increase. Under these assumptions, individual countries could gain by expanding their exports, but all developing countries could not do so. Correspondingly, the limited possibilities of expanding the exports of primary products would appear as a constraint to the acceleration of economic growth in less developed areas.

This conclusion should be qualified by considering that in the production of a number of commodities, developing countries compete with developed economies

67

on the world market, and hence the price elasticity of demand for their exports may exceed unity. On the other hand, it should be recalled that, especially in the field of agriculture, developed countries often rely on policies of price support *cum* export subsidies so as to maintain the share of home production in domestic and foreign markets.

Should market limitations not permit an acceleration of economic growth in less developed countries through the expansion of their exports of primary products, increases in the exports of manufactures and import substitution can serve as alternative strategies. More generally, in the framework of national markets, economic growth can proceed through the exportation of primary goods, exports of manufactured goods, and import substitution. The first of these alternatives found application in Australia, New Zealand, Canada, and Denmark; the second in the United Kingdom at the time of the Industrial Revolution, while a combination of the second and the third appears to have been operative in Germany, France and Japan.

In the previous lecture, I indicated that the prospects for the exports of primary producing countries largely depend on the composition of their exports. By and large, the prospects appear to be favorable for the exporters of minerals and metals, while the expectations of countries that specialize in agricultural products are generally rather poor. Correspondingly, although export earnings will not constrain economic growth in the Middle East, Venezuela, and much of North Africa, the majority of the countries of Latin America, tropical Africa, and Asia can hardly rely on exports of primary products for improving their past growth performance. The question arises, then, whether the exportation of manufactured goods and/or import substitution can be possible avenues for the acceleration of economic growth in these national economies.

EXPORTATION OF MANUFACTURED GOODS FROM LESS DEVELOPED AREAS

As regards manufactured goods, the possibilities for increasing the exportation of simple manufactures, such as textiles, jute goods, leather, and plywood and veneer, should first be examined. These products have the common characteristics that their manufacturing does not require sophisticated technical know-how and the existence of interrelated industries, capital requirements are usually modest, and the manufacturing process is either labor-intensive or it utilizes domestic materials.

It appears that countries with cheap labor or materials could expand their exports of manufactured goods, and the comparative advantage of countries presently specializing in agricultural products for which demand is rising at a slow rate would increasingly lie in labor —and material— intensive manufactures. The exports of manufactures from less developed areas increased at a rapid rate during the fifties although their share hardly surpassed five per cent of the total exports of the developing countries in 1960. Moreover, in recent years, a slackening in the expansion of these exports has been experienced. Various measures taken by developed as well as by developing countries have contributed to this result.

To begin with, exports of cotton textiles from India and Hong Kong that had been growing rapidly during the fifties, and came to account for one-third of the manufactured exports of developing countries, were subjected to formal or informal quotas in 1960. As a result of the imposition of quotas, increases in exports were negligible in the two years following. The International Cotton Textiles Agreement provides for future increases in exports, although the proportion of the textile consumption of developed economies supplied by developing countries would remain relatively modest. Thus, in the United States and the Common Market countries, who imported about 1 per cent of all domestically consumed cotton goods from less developed countries in 1960, this proportion would not surpass 2 and 3 per cent, respectively, even if the International Cotton Textiles Agreement were to be extended until 1975. And U. S. imports may, in fact, rise at a slower rate than envisaged, given that the United States has already invoked the "market disruption" clause of the Agreement.

Quotas on cotton textiles, as well as quantitative restrictions applied in a number of European countries on jute goods, sewing machines, bicycles, and sports goods originating in less developed areas, not only limit the exportation of these commodities, but also create an unfavorable climate for the exports of other manufactures from developing economies. Entrepreneurs in less developed countries, who have witnessed the imposition of restrictions on commodities, the foreign sales of which expanded at a rapid rate, may well assume that other manufactured goods will receive similar treatment if and when these come to be exported in larger quantities. Correspondingly, entrepreneurial calculations are likely to include an allowance for the risk associated with the possible application of trade restrictions in the developed countries, and this fact may discourage investment in new facilities for purposes of exportation.

The "graduation" of tariffs in the main industrial countries provides a further disincentive to the exportation of manufactured goods from less developed areas. By graduated tariffs, I mean the progression of tariff rates according to the degree of fabrication as observed with respect to a wide variety of commodities, including cocoa, coffee, oilseeds and vegetable oils, leather, rubber, lumber, paper, cotton, wool, jute, and metals. In the case of these commodities, duties are low or nonexistent for raw materials, and the level of duty generally increases with the level of fabrication. In the European Common Market, for example, there is no duty on hides and skins, a 10 per cent tariff is applied to leather, and 17-20 per cent of leather manufactures, while in the case of cocoa the progression of tariffs is 5.6 per cent on cocoa beans, 22 per cent on cocoa butter, 25 per cent on cocoa paste, and 27 per cent on cocoa powder. Similar instances are observed in the United States and the United Kingdom, too.

At the same time, the disincentive effect of graduated tariffs is only imperfectly indicated by a comparison of tariff levels since, from the point of view of the entrepreneur, not differences in rates of duty but the ratio of the increment in duty to value added in the manufacturing process is relevant. Thus, an increase in the rate of tariff from 5 per cent on the raw material to 10 per cent on the processed commodity will represent a 15 per cent duty on value added if the raw material accounts for one-half of the final price.

The graduation of tariffs from raw materials to semi-processed and processed goods does not continue, however, as we move to more sophisticated products. Tariff rates rise from iron ore to pig iron to steel ingots, and to finished articles of steel, for example, but duties again become lower on much of machinery and transport equipment. Relatively low duties on highly sophisticated products manufactured chiefly in industrial economies, as compared to the simple manufactures exported by developing countries, are the result of the system of tariff-bargaining carried out in the framework of GATT where concessions have been traded for concessions on a com-

71

modity-by-commodity basis. The U. S. Trade Expansion Act empowered the President to negotiate tariff reductions for broad commodity groups rather than individual commodities, but the observed disparities in tariffs are likely to increase rather than diminish. According to the provisions of the Act, tariffs could be eliminated on commodities where the United States and the European Common Market countries supply over 80 per cent of world exports, while for the remaining groups of commodities —where presumably the interests of the developing countries lie— the negotiating authority has been given for a 50 per cent tariff-cut only.

At the same time, possibilities for the manufacturing of more sophisticated products within the narrow national markets of the less developed countries are greatly limited. The manufacturing of these products requires technical and organizational skills that are often not available in the less developed countries and, more importantly, the production of many of these commodities presupposes the existence of a highly developed industrial structure with all its interindustry relationships.

But developed countries should not shoulder all the blame for the relatively small volume of the exports of simple manufactures from developing economies, since measures undertaken by the latter often provide disincentives to exportation. In a number of Latin American countries, for example, the overvaluation of exchange rates and preferential tax treatment given to the production of import substitutes have had such an effect. At the same time, high tariffs and other trade barriers have restricted the exchange of manufactured goods among the less developed countries themselves. These considerations bring us to our next topic, the possibilities for import substitution in the less developed countries.

With the relatively slow growth of export earnings and the desire to accelerate the rate of economic growth in the countries of Latin America and Asia, efforts have been made to substitute domestic products for imports in a variety of industries producing chiefly nondurable consumer goods. While import substitution has contributed to economic growth in several of these countries, it has frequently been misdirected. For one thing, countries often followed "beggar-my-neighbor" policies by substituting domestic production for commodities previously imported from their neighbors; for another, efforts have frequently been made to produce at home whatever possible with no regard to cost. Raul Prebisch notes that "the criterion by which the choice was determined was based not on considerations of economic expediency, but on immediate feasibility, whatever the cost of production".[1] This result has been achieved chiefly by the application of high tariffs (often 300-400 per cent), exchange restrictions, and tax concessions in Latin America, and the imposition of quotas in Asia.

Although in the presence of overvalued exchange rates and a wide variety of restrictive measures, meaningful estimates of the cost of protection cannot be made, it may be suggested that, at least in the case of Latin America, the height of tariffs provides some indication of the cost of protection. Under competitive conditions, the tariff equals the difference between the marginal cost of domestic production and the world market price, and indicates the cost of protection to the consumer. On the other hand, while the excess cost to the consumer reflects losses due to the misallocation of resources under competitive conditions, part of this cost takes the form

---

[1] Raúl Prebisch, *Towards a Dynamic Development Policy for Latin America*, New York, United Nations, 1963, p. 71.

of monopoly profits in the case of monopolistic market structures. The latter is by no means uncommon in less developed areas. In the framework of narrow national markets, one or two firms often provide for domestic demand and —in the absence of foreign competition— these firms follow a policy of small turnover and high profit per unit of output.

A further consideration is that tariff protection behind national frontiers has not permitted intra-regional competition and specialization in newly created industries. At the same time, the inefficiencies due to the lack of competition and specialization have been compounded by reason of the fact that economies of scale have been foregone in industries established behind national tariff walls.

These considerations suggest the inadequacies of the present system of protection. At the same time, import substitution can hardly proceed at the rates observed in the last decade. To cite Prebisch again, "the stage of easy substitution is past. It was relatively simple to substitute domestic production for imports of individual items of current consumption and of some durable consumer and capital goods, and there is little margin left for substitution in this field in most of Latin America. We are now moving into the stage of import substitution in respect of intermediate products or durable consumer or capital goods, which, besides being difficult to manufacture, require markets much larger than those of the individual Latin American countries".[2] Similar conclusions have been reached in Asia where the present amount of imports from outside the region is considered to be near to the "minimum level of economic feasibility" in most countries.[3]

[2] Op. cit., p. 69.
[3] United Nations, Economic Comission for Asia and the Far East, Economic Bulletin for Asia and the Far East, December, 1961, p. 49.

74

I have discussed today some problems relating to the acceleration of economic growth through larger exports or import replacement in less developed countries. The relevant questions can be reformulated by stating that countries which have limited possibilities for raising their primary products exports face two possible choices under present-day conditions: the parallel development of a number of industries and concentrated growth of a few branches of manufacturing. Both of these choices have their advantages and disadvantages.

Parallel advance along a broad front would make it possible to enjoy external economies operating through input-output relationships and via income changes. As regards the first, I have previously used the example of the steel industry, the expansion of which will increase demand for iron ore and coal, and may also provide cheaper inputs for steel using industries. Increased demand for iron ore and coal can, then, lead to greater mechanization in mining, and cheaper steel may induce entrepreneurs in steel using industries to reconsider their production methods. It should be added that the steel industry, in turn, would benefit from an expansion in the production of coal and iron ore and in steel using industries, through lower costs and larger sales. Thus, a simultaneous expansion of interrelated industries will not only contribute to the employment of previously unutilized resources, if any, but it can also give rise to the application of more advanced methods of production.

Another form of external economies operates through income changes. As Rosenstein-Rodan and Nurkse noted, the parallel expansion in a number of consumer goods industries would create markets for the products of each, and, at the same time, it would make possible the installation of plants of efficient size in all industries. These results would thus reinforce the effects of the simultaneous development of interrelated industries on economic growth.

But parallel expansion in a number of industries encounters limitations on the supply side as well as on the demand side in the less developed countries of today. While labor may be abundant in many of these countries, this can hardly be said about capital and entrepreneurs. The limited availability of these factors will then create obstacles to parallel advance along a broad front.

The small size of national markets provides a further limitation. Industries for the products of which home demand is not sufficient to warrant the installation of domestic plants in less developed countries, include various chemicals, electronics, special metal products, and heavy machinery. In Mexico, for example, although there is demand for coal derivatives in the production of resins, paint, coatings, insecticides and dyes, the small national market does not allow for the establishment of domestic plants.

In other cases, economies of scale are foregone either because plants are built at less than optimum size, or because they manufacture a large variety of products instead of concentrating on a few lines of production. The steel industry, the production of fertilizers, and the manufacturing of pulp and paper are examples for the former, textiles and metal products for the latter.

Instead of installing small, inefficient plants, some developing countries build ahead of demand, and set up modern plants which will have to operate at less than full capacity for a prolonged period. These industries may escape the excess cost incurred in small scale production, but building ahead of demand, too, involves an economic cost inasmuch as a scarce resource, capital, is not fully utilized.

The existence of excess capacity has been observed

76

in a large number of industries of the more advanced Latin American countries. It has been reported, for example, that in 1962 in Mexico iron foundries worked at 50 per cent capacity, cigarette factories at 78 per cent, and textile plants at 42 per cent. The production of railroad cars, refrigerators, TV sets, and electrical appliances are further examples. Similar instances can be found in Brazil and Argentina.

Finally, even if the establishment of an efficient plant were possible in individual industries, the economies of intra-industry specialization could hardly be enjoyed. Present-day developing countries are not able to produce various parts, components, and accessories for machinery and consumer durables on an optimum scale, for example, and will not sustain the operation of certain subsidiary activities. Thus, in developing countries that have embarked on the manufacture of automobiles, automobile plants usually produce also various components and accessories, such as electrical and ignition' systems, spark plugs, heaters, steering wheels, springs, and the lack of specialization entails higher costs.

Prospects for Concentrated Growth

If supply limitations do not permit the exploitation of economies of scale in the case of a parallel development of a number of industries, this would not be the case if expansion were concentrated in a few branches of manufacturing. Concentrated growth may also be conducive to technological progress since the rapid expansion of output would allow for the introduction of new technological methods. It faces obstacles from the side of demand, however, since it is hardly compatible with the existence of narrow national markets.

To escape the market-imposed limitations, countries concentrating on a few industries would have to export a large proportion of their output. At the same time, in the absence of external economies obtainable through interindustry relationships, the competitiveness of these industries will suffer, and in cases when they are competitive, trade restrictions and uncertainty in foreign trade interfere with the expansion of exports to other developing economies as well as to developed countries.

I have noted earlier in this lecture that tariffs in developing countries are usually the highest on commodities a country produces —or desires to produce— domestically, and high tariffs and other forms of restrictions limit trade in manufactured goods among the developing countries. Under present structures, existing trade in these commodities may, in fact, decline in years to come, inasmuch as countries in Africa and Southeast Asia, that have been importing textiles from India and Hong Kong, are now aiming at self-sufficiency.

I have also made reference to the effects of restrictions prevailing in the industrial countries on imports of manufactured goods from less developed areas. To illustrate the importance of these factors, we can compare the case of Puerto Rico to that of other Latin American countries. Puerto Rico is poor in natural resources in comparison with Venezuela or Chile but it has the important advantage over the latter in that her products can freely enter the U. S. market. Puerto Rican products are not subject to tariffs in the U. S. markets, and there is no exchange risk or uncertainty concerning the future imposition of restrictions. These factors have contributed to the establishment of industries in Puerto Rico that would have natural advantages elsewhere, such as the petrochemical industry in Venezuela, since the availability and the certainty of the U. S. market have outweighed considerations of natural advantages.

It appears then that, in the presence of limited possibilities for the exportation of manufactured goods, the size of domestic markets appears as a constraint for present-day developing countries in the case of the parallel expansion of a number of industries as well as for concentrated growth. This conclusion leads us back to the problem as to how market size is to be measured. For purposes of indicating the possibilities for the reallocation of resources in an integrated area, I have proposed to measure market size as the volume of production excluding the subsistence sector, with further consideration given to differences in tastes and transportation costs. In order to indicate the possibilities of reaping economies of scale and external economies, we should also exclude agricultural production and personal services from the scope of the definition, since in the latter sectors increases in market size will have little effect on productivity.

Correspondingly, for present purposes, the consumption of industrial goods could provide an indicator of market size. But data on the consumption of manufactured products in less developed countries are not readily available and we have to rely on some other, necessarily crude, indicators instead. As a first step, a comparison of gross national products and per capita incomes may be useful, when account should be taken of the fact that the demand for manufactured goods increases more rapidly than per capita incomes —especially in countries with low living standards.

As a standard of comparison, let us take Germany, France, and the United Kingdom, the gross national product of which —converted by utilizing purchasing power parities rather than exchange rates— is about U.S. $ 70-80 billion a year, and per capita GNP around $ 1 400-

79

1 500. We find that, even in the largest developing countries, India and Brazil, the gross national product does not exceed $ 60 and $ 25 billion, and, more importantly, per capita incomes amount to $ 140 and $ 370 in the two countries, respectively. The corresponding data for Mexico and Pakistan, the next two countries in line, are $ 15 and $ 11 billion for the gross national product, and $ 410 and $ 120 for per capita incomes. Per capita incomes in Africa are even lower than in Asia, and the two largest countries here, Egypt and Nigeria, have a gross national product of $ 6.0 and $ 4.7 billion, respectively.[4]

Further consideration should be given to existing inequalities in incomes in the less developed countries. In Mexico, for example, the country that appears to have reached the highest average per capita income level among less developed countries, other than the oil-producing states, the urban poor and the ejido farmer, who make up from $2/3$ to $3/4$ of the population, fall outside the market for a wide range of industrial products. The inequalities of income distribution, the small share of industrial products in the family budget at low income levels, and the difficulties of transportation and communication in the larger underdeveloped countries all indicate the limitations of national markets for manufactured goods.

It would appear, then, that in countries that are large in terms of population and, in some cases, also in terms of national incomes, the effective market for industrial goods, in the production of which large-scale economies can be obtained, is rather small. In fact, in none of these countries does the market for durable and a number of

---

[4] GNP estimates for developing countries have again been taken from Rosenstein-Rodan, *Review of Economics and Statistics* paper, while those for developed countries have been derived from my *Trade Prospects for Developing Countries*.

nondurable goods reach that of a country like Belgium or the Netherlands, the latter of which have a gross national product of $ 15 billion and per capita incomes of $ 1 300-1 500.

These conclusions are supported by empirical evidence on the consumption of individual commodities for which comparable data are available. Steel consumption in Brazil was 2.7 million tons and in Argentina 2.4 million tons in 1961, for example, as against 3.3 million tons in Belgium and 3.2 million tons in the Netherlands. In the same year, Belgium had over 0.8 million, and the Netherlands 0.6 million of automobiles, as compared to 0.5-0.6 million in Argentina and Brazil, and yet the former countries did not engage in car production while the latter established a number of plants behind productive tariff walls.

INTEGRATION: REMEDY OR PANACEA?

We may now conclude that, under present-day conditions, less developed countries face certain handicaps in attempting to accelerate their economic growth. The possibilities for expanding their exports of primary products and manufactures are often limited, and they encounter barriers in the process of import substitution, too. While import substitution has been an important factor contributing to economic growth in many of the developing countries in the last decade, this has often necessitated a high degree of protection, and protection entails an economic cost. On the one hand, it leads to the establishment of inefficient firms and monopolistic market structures; on the other, in narrow national markets, large-scale economies are foregone or excess capacity generated. At the same time, import substitution becomes increasingly difficult and costly after imports of simple manufactures have been replaced by home products.

In turn, integration can contribute to more efficient resource allocation and to the exploitation of internal and external economies. Resources will be allocated more efficiently after the removal of internal trade barriers that have obstructed the exchange of commodities among developing countries. The establishment of a free trade area or customs union will also permit reaping economies of scale, since the effective size of the market will increase as the number of people with similar income levels rises. Further gains can be obtained as external economies derived from interindustry relationships in production and consumption are appropriated in a wider market. Finally, it is expected that in existing industries the monopoly power of firms protected by national tariff barriers would be reduced in the integrated area.

Economic integration in less developed areas would thus provide opportunities for the parallel development of a number of industries, accompanied by the exploitation of economies of scale. Integration is not a panacea, however. By enlarging the market it can provide a suitable framework for economic growth but the results will greatly depend on the economic policies to be followed. To appropriate the large scale economies attainable in an integrated area, for example, increased investments are necessary which will not be forthcoming if foreign investment is discouraged and domestic savings are not generated. Also, changes in the social structure will often be called for in the process of economic development, and appropriate policies will have to be devised in cases when the area is not large enough to support several producers in a given industry.

ECONOMIC INTEGRATION AND PROTECTIONISM

It has often been charged that integration would lead
to the establishment of a high cost area and, especially
in less developed regions, it is basically a protectionist
device. This argument is based on two, often unstated,
assumptions. On the one hand, it presupposes the possibility of accelerating economic growth through the
expansion of exports; on the other, it assumes that a
policy of import substitution would not be followed by
individual national economies.

But less developed countries that rely on the exportation of agricultural products can hardly expect to speed
up their economic growth by expanding their traditional
exports. At the same time, past experience as well as
plans prepared in less developed countries indicate that
these countries are pursuing a policy of import substitution behind national frontiers. The choice is therefore
not so much between free trade and import substitution in an integrated area, as between import substitution within national frontiers or in the framework of
a free trade area (customs union).

Our previous considerations indicate that the cost
of import substitution in terms of alternatives foregone
will decrease in a free trade area or a customs union
where improvements in resource allocation and cost
reductions due to internal and external economies can
be obtained. The reduction in the cost of protection, in
turn, provides possibilities for a more rational policy
of industrialization. Ultimately, non-participating countries may benefit through an increased exchange of industrial products. H. B. Chenery's intercountry comparisons indicate, for example, that while industrialization entails a rise in manufacturing production far
exceeding increases in imports, the share of industrial

83

imports in national income declines but little.[5] With the
acceleration of economic growth following integration,
the imports of less developed areas may then eventually
reach a level higher than that attainable without integration.

[5] "Patterns of Industrial Growth", *American Economic Review*, September 1960, pp. 640-42.

CHAPTER IV

LARGE SCALE ECONOMIES AND INTEGRATION

INTRA-INDUSTRY ECONOMIES OF LARGE-SCALE PRODUCTION

In the last lecture, I examined the role of external economies operating through interindustry relationships and income changes in a union of developing countries. Aside from the utilization of hitherto unused resources, these external economies generally involve the exploitation of increasing returns to scale in individual industries, a fact which lends special interest to a consideration of the possibilities for intraindustry economies. That will be our topic today.

An enlargement of the market will have a three-fold effect on the operation of individual industries. First, as the size of the market size increases, larger plants, or combinations of plants, will be built, provided that a lowering of costs is attained thereby. This is economies of scale in a narrower sense, and when using the word, we usually refer to this one (economies of scale proper). Second, a widening of the market will make possible the reduction of product variety in individual plants, accompanied by a lengthening of the production runs. Third, in a larger market, various activities can be separated in individual plants. Thus, instead of producing, for example, automobiles with all their parts, components, and accessories in one plant, the latter can be manufactured in separate establishments.

In other words, an increase in the size of the market allows for the establishment of larger plants as well as for horizontal and vertical specialization. By horizontal specialization we mean that firms specialize in different varieties of the same commodity, while vertical specialization refers to separating various activities leading to the production of a given commodity in individual establishments. I have elsewhere used the simile that "this process can be visualized by imagining a growing plant producing various intermediate and final products, when a further extension of operation would result in the continuous splitting-up of the plant in vertical and horizontal directions".[1] The automobile industry can again be used as an example where firms not only set up plants to produce various parts, accessories and components, but individual models, such as Ford and Mercury, have also come to be produced in separate plants.

In the process of horizontal and vertical specialization, all newly established plants can enjoy economies of scale but they may be smaller in size than the original, nonspecialized plant. This conclusion indicates the difficulty of comparing plant sizes.

In attempting to assess the possibilities of obtaining economies of scale in East Africa, Brown suggested to estimate the number of efficient plants the East African market would support, by comparing the consumption of manufactured goods in this area to the median size of plants in British industries.[2] But, while this method may be applicable in the case of homogeneous commodities, such as cement, it leads to misleading results in regard to cotton textiles, footwear and other consumer and producer goods where product differentiation is prevalent.

In the latter instances, the efficient operation of a

[1] Bela Balassa, *The Theory of Economic Integration*, p. 127.
[2] A. J. Brown, "Economic Separatism versus a Common Market in Developing Countries", *Yorkshire Bulletin of Economic and Social Research*, May 1961, pp. 33-40 and November 1961, pp. 86-96.

median British plant presupposes its integration into an industry manufacturing heterogeneous products, with individual plants specializing in different varieties of the same commodity. Thus, while the consumption of footwear in an underdeveloped country might equal the production of a median British establishment, efficient production could still not be ensured in such a country since its only plant would have to produce all kinds of footwear in use rather than one or two varieties. Considering also the cost reductions associated with vertical specialization, it becomes apparent that the three types of economies of scale have to be examined individually, in order to provide an indication of the gains from large-scale economies obtainable in a union of developing economies.

PLANT SIZE AND ECONOMIES OF SCALE

Economies of scale proper can be classified in their relationship to indivisibilities, capacity-cost ratios, nonproportional activities, and the application of advanced technological methods. Among these, indivisibilities may pertain to a single unit of equipment that is necessary to produce a certain commodity, or, alternatively, several units of an indivisible equipment may be called for. In the latter case, optimal operation requires that the plant's capacity should equal some common multiple of the capacities of units of efficient size.

Economies of scale result from a technological relationship between capacity and costs in the case of containers, pipelines, compressors, etc., where cost is a function of the surface area while capacity is related to volume. The loss of heat or energy in furnaces and electric conductors is also related to the surface area while increases in capacity are proportional to volume. On the basis of these relationships, engineers have derived the so-called .6 rule, according to which a 10 per cent increase in capacity would be accompanied by an approximately 6 per cent rise in costs.

Economies of scale can also be obtained in conjunction with various non-proportional activities, such as design, production planning, research, channeling and collecting information, handling, shipping, and repair facilities. In general, we find that, at higher levels of output, the per-unit cost of these activities tends to decline. At the same time, in view of the operation of the law of large numbers, inventory holdings of spare parts and final products, as well as cash balances, need to increase less than proportionally as output expands. Finally, larger plant size may allow for the application of advanced technological methods that entail the use of specialized equipment and assembly-line production, and can also lead to the specialization of workers and management.

The relative importance of these forms of economies of scale and the magnitudes of cost reductions at higher levels of output will differ among industries. In the following, I will examine the available evidence for several industries that are of interest to the developing countries. The evidence presented has been derived from engineering estimates pertaining to the manufacturing of homogeneous products where direct comparisons can be made.

Petroleum Refining and Chemicals

The .6 rule finds application in petroleum refining where the existence of economies of scale has been, in part, responsible for the establishment of refineries in the main consuming centers of North America and Western Europe. The chemical industry provides further examples, among which we may single out the production of

90

fertilizers that have special importance for developing countries, where increases in fertilizer production are a precondition for the introduction of modern agricultural methods.

In the manufacture of fertilizers, economies of scale can be obtained by reason of the less than proportionate rise in inputs with increases in output and the application of the "law of multiples" in combining the production of ammonia and that of fertilizers. As regards the first, it has been shown that a doubling of the output of ammonia involves a 40 per cent increase in labor costs and 81 per cent rise in capital costs, while the relevant figures for ammonium nitrate and ammonium sulphate —the two most important types of fertilizers— are 27 and 68 per cent, and 20 and 65 per cent, respectively.

With consideration given also to transportation costs, Vietorisz and Manne[3] have found that the estimated fertilizer needs of Latin American countries in the year 1965 could be most efficiently supplied by a single integrated plant. The cost of the optimal combination for an annual production of 1 million tons of ammonia has been given as U.S. $ 64.9 million as against $ 89.4 million in the case of the "noncooperative solution" when intra-area trade is assumed to be nil, whereas the cost of fully relying on imports from outside the area would exceed $ 100 million. The construction of a second fertilizer plant —to be supplied by ammonia produced at the first location— would become desirable only after Latin American fertilizer consumption will have reached nearly twice the projected 1965 level, and consumption would have to more than double to warrant the establishment

[3] Thomas Vietorisz and Alan S. Manne, "Chemical Processes, Plant Location, and Economies of Scale", *Studies in Process Analysis*, ed. A. S. Manne and H. M. Markowitz, New York, John Wiley & Sons, 1963, pp. 136-58.

of a second plant producing ammonia. These conclusions apply, *mutatis mutandis*, to Asia and Africa. At the same time, in the absence of economic integration, fertilizer plants are constructed in these areas to produce at a scale substantially smaller than that indicated above.

STEEL

Economies of scale can be obtained also in the production of steel. According to information provided in an ECLA publication, *A Study of the Iron and Steel Industry in Latin America*, over 1 million ingot tons is the annual output of an integrated steel plant of efficient size, costs are approximately 18 per cent higher at capacity levels of 0.5 million tons and 33 per cent higher in a plant producing 0.25 million tons per year. Yet, among less developed countries, steel production exceeds 1.0 million tons a year only in India, Brazil, and Mexico, while annual production is below 0.5 million tons in Argentina, Chile, Colombia, South Korea, Pakistan, and Rhodesia.

The method employed by Vietorisz and Manne for fertilizers has been utilized by a student in my economic integration seminar at Yale, Mrs. Materina-Mantel, for determining the optimum pattern of steel production in Latin America for the year 1970. The Instituto Latinoamericano del Fierro y del Acero estimated steel consumption in the five countries under consideration (Argentina, Brazil, Chile, Mexico, and Venezuela) to amount to 13 million metric tons of steel in 1970, while production costs have been estimated to increase by 7.4 per cent for a 10 per cent rise in output. With appropriate consideration given to transportation costs and inter-country differences in the availability of coal and iron ore, Mrs. Mantel concluded that the optimum pattern of production would entail Mexico and Chile supplying

92

steel to the other countries considered. Similar calculations have not been made for Asia and Africa, but available information suggests that an efficient pattern of production would involve locating steel mills in one or at most two countries of these areas.

PULP AND PAPER

Indivisibilities and capacity-cost ratios account for economies of scale in pulp and paper manufacturing. The establishment of pulp and paper mills is of special importance for the less developed countries since, despite their favorable resource endowments, these economies have an overall deficit in pulp and paper. According to the FAO, present expansion plans indicate a continuation of this deficit, so that net imports of pulp into the less developed countries would amount to 0.90 million tons in 1965, and of paper and newsprint to 1.43 million tons. These imports would require a foreign exchange expenditure of nearly $0.5 billion.[4]

The raw material for pulp and paper making, timber, is available in the less developed areas in abundance, although it would be desirable to grow homogeneous timber that is more amenable for processing. In Latin America, for example, excellent possibilities for the expansion of timber production exist in Chile, in Mexico, and in the Amazon region of Brazil. Still, expansion has been restricted by reason of the large capital and foreign exchange needs of efficient size plants and the low volume of intra-area trade.

The importance of economies of scale in pulp and paper manufacturing is indicated by a comparison of production costs at various capacity levels and the world market price f. o. b. mill in Table 5. It appears that at

[4] Food and Agriculture Organization, *World Demand for Paper to 1975*, Rome, 1962, pp. 63-65.

TABLE 5

LATIN AMERICA: UNIT COSTS AND PRICES
PER METRIC TON, U.S.$

Product	Capacity (tons per day)	Capital charges	Direct cost	Total cost	Mill net price [1]
Bleached Kraft	50	82	167	249	130
Pulp	100	58	127	185	130
	200	44	105	149	130
Bleached Kraft	50	108	200	308	190
Pulp and Paper	100	73	150	223	190
	200	56	123	179	190
Newsprint	50	72	150	222	125
	100	48	119	167	125
	200	36	101	137	125

SOURCE: *Programming Data and Criteria for the Pulp and Paper Industry*, United Nations ST/ECLA/CONF. 11/L. 19. December 19, 1962.
[1] Mill net price = Approximate world price less allowances for selling and freight expenses.

capacity levels of 50 thousand tons a day, pulp and paper mills operate at a unit cost 60-80 per cent higher than the net world market price, and the latter is approached only in mills with a daily capacity of 200 tons. Costs decline further as capacity increases, the decrease being approximately 15 per cent between the 200 and the 500 ton level.

At the same time, mills with a daily output of less than 50 tons per day are the rule rather than the exception in the less developed countries. In fact, among these countries, total installed capacity in pulp production exceeded daily 100 tons in 1958 only in India, Argentina, Brazil, and Chile. Economic integration can, then, lead to a reduction in costs of expansion of pulp and paper manufacturing in countries where production conditions are the most favorable. While detailed information on plant capacities and raw material costs in the various countries is not available, it may be of interest to indicate differences in the cost of setting up mills to remove the prospective deficit of the Latin American area in pulp and paper under varying assumptions as to plant size.

According to calculations carried out by Oscar Muñoz in my integration seminar, an increase in productive capacity that would eliminate the prospective Latin American deficit of 470 thousand tons in newsprint estimated for the year 1965, would necessitate an investment of U.S. $202 million if mills with a daily capacity of 50 tons were built, $135 million in case of mills producing 100 tons, and $101 million in case of mills producing 200 tons a day. The $100 million saving in investment costs attainable by building 200 tons instead of 50 tons mills would be accompanied by a saving in operating cost of about 33 per cent. For pulp and paper mills the relevant figures are $70 million and 38 per cent.

The construction of larger mills would also reduce foreign exchange recovery time. For wood-pulp this would fall from 5.3 in the case of mills with a daily capacity of 50 tons to 1.8 for mills producing 200 tons and 1.6 for mills producing 300 tons a day. Reductions of similar magnitude could be obtained in regard to paper, while differences are somewhat smaller in the case of newsprint. These results are of special importance if we consider that about 60-70 per cent of the cost of building a pulp or paper mill involves a foreign exchange expenditure.

OTHER MANUFACTURES

Economies of scale obtainable in the production of synthetic fibers should further be mentioned. According to information provided by J. S. Bain, optimal operation

95

in rayon yarn manufacturing requires an annual output of 20-25 thousand tons, while costs increase 8 per cent for a plant half of this size and 15 per cent in a plant with one quarter of optimal output.[5] At the same time, among less developed countries, annual output exceeds 20 thousand tons only in Brazil and India, it is 14 thousand tons in Mexico, 5-10 thousand tons in Argentina and the United Arab Republic, and below 5 thousand tons in Chile, Colombia, Peru, Uruguay, and Venezuela.

Economies of scale may also be obtained in the production of metals, transport equipment, machinery, consumer durables, cement, and several other products.[6] But economies of scale proper can be appropriately estimated only in the case of industries that manufacture homogeneous products while the difficulties encountered in the comparison of plant sizes hinder reaching conclusions with respect to the manufacturing of heterogeneous commodities. In the latter instances, economies of scale in the form of horizontal and vertical specialization assume importance.

HORIZONTAL SPECIALIZATION

In industries producing a great variety of commodities, plants in larger countries are generally able to specialize in a narrower range of commodities and enjoy cost advantages due to longer production runs. These cost advantages relate to reductions in fixed cost per unit, decreases in some elements of direct costs, and increased productivity at higher output levels.

A lengthening of the production run may entail re-

[5] J. S. Bain, *Barriers to New Competition*, Cambridge, Mass., Harvard University Press, 1958, ch. III.

[6] Information on economies of scale in these industries is given in Bain's above-mentioned study as well as in ch. 6 of my work *The Theory of Economic Integration*.

ductions in fixed costs per unit of output through the use of specialized machinery and by reason of the lower costs involved in making molds, preparing designs, etc. Savings in fixed costs are of special importance in the metal-working and machine-tool industries, although examples can also be found in various branches of engineering.

Longer production runs also contribute to a lowering of certain direct costs. These include the expense associated with resetting machines, reorganizing work, and shifting labor from one operation to another. Besides the industries mentioned above, the direct cost of changeover assumes importance in the textile industry and in the production of some chemicals. With regard to the latter, the cost of set-up and clean-up operations in the manufacturing of pharmaceuticals, dyes, and various organic chemicals may be mentioned.

Last but not least, in the case of short production runs potential improvements in manufacturing efficiency are foregone. Estimates made for several industries indicated improvements in productivity along the "learning curve" as output rises. In several industries this gain has been put at 15-20 per cent as output doubles, although one could not expect it to continue indefinitely. The manufacturing of airframes, machine tools, and shipbuilding are examples.[7]

It has been suggested that, in explaining productivity differentials between the United States and Western Europe, differences in the length of the production run may be of greater importance than differences in plant sizes.[8] Available information does not permit us to eva-

---

[7] W. Z. Hirsch, "Manufacturing Progress Functions", *Review of Economics and Statistics*, May 1952, pp. 143-53, and Harold Asher, *Cost-quantity Relationships in the Airframe Industry*, Santa Monica, Cal., The RAND Corporation, 1956.

[8] P. J. Verdoorn in *Economic Consequences of the Size of Nations*, Robinson, E. A. G. (ed.), London, Macmillan, 1960, p. 346.

luate this claim, however, and neither can we provide a quantitative appraisal of gains to be attained from standardization in present-day developing countries. For one thing, in the latter countries, several of the industries in question have not yet been established or are still in their infancy; for another, few estimates of gains derived from the lengthening of production runs are available. Still, some indications can be given in the possibilities for productivity improvements in the textile industries of the less developed countries.

Among manufacturing industries, the production of textiles is usually the first to be undertaken in developing economies. At the same time, with the outstanding exceptions of India and Hong Kong, textile factories have been established in highly protected national markets and these have little possibilities for exportation. Textile industries have sprung up in almost all countries of Latin America and Asia and, more recently, the production of textiles has been begun in some African countries, too.

Economies of scale proper appear to be of relatively small importance in the textile industry; according to estimates by ECLA, costs per unit decrease by about 10 per cent as output doubles.[9] But further improvements can be obtained by reducing the variety of products presently manufactured in the textile plants of the less developed countries, considering that in the presence of often prohibitive restrictions on international exchange, firms in individual countries endeavor to provide a full assortment of products. Potential gains can be illustrated by reference to U. S.-Canadian comparisons.

According to information provided by firms operating in both the United States and Canada, higher manufacturing efficiency in the former as compared to the

[9] ST/ECLA/CONF. 11/L. 20.

98

latter can be explained by the fact that in the larger American market plants can specialize in one type of fabric while Canadian mills often produce 5 to 100 types of fabrics. These conclusions apply *a fortiori* to the textile industries of less developed countries since production in most of these countries takes place on a scale considerably smaller than in Canada.

VERTICAL SPECIALIZATION

I come now to economies of scale that can be obtained as an enlargement of the market leads to changes in the structure of individual industries, involving the segregation of various operations in separate undertakings. This process of vertical specialization will contribute to greater productivity, inasmuch as economies of scale can be appropriated in the specialized plants.

Gains from vertical specialization appear at various levels of industrial development. In chronological order, the tanning industry might have provided the first example of this process in present-day industrial economies, followed by the printing trade, the metal industry, machine building, and in the first decades of this century, the automobile industry. But the process of intra-industry specialization is far from completed, and even in countries such as Britain further gains can be obtained from specialization following an enlargement of the market. As C. F. Carter and B. R. Williams noted, "in certain industries the British market has not been big enough to encourage the growth of specialist producers of equipment —who themselves might have created new possibilities of progress".[10]

Industries mentioned in regard to Britain are fine chemicals, plastics, rubber, aircraft, and scientific ins-

[10] *Industry and Technical Progress*, London, Oxford University Press, 1957, p. 155.

99

LEWIS AND CLARK COLLEGE LIBRARY
PORTLAND, OREGON   97219

truments. The range of the relevant industries is considerably wider in present-day underdeveloped economies that can follow the example of developed countries in obtaining the benefits of intra-industry specialization in a number of industries. These include, among others, metal manufacturing and the automobile industry.

Metal manufacturing has often been cited as an example of vertical and horizontal specialization in describing developments in Europe during the latter half of the nineteenth century. It has been noted that, with the expansion of this industry, plants have come to specialize vertically in foundry, casting, forging, and toolmaking; and horizontally, in the manufacture of needles and pins, safes and locks, domestic hollow ware, and more recently in electric heat and cooking apparatus, batteries, etc. The advantages of specialization can be enjoyed in a union of less developed countries, in many of which metal manufacturing is in its infancy.

While horizontal and vertical specialization are characteristic of metal manufacturing, economies of scale proper and vertical specialization are of importance in the production of automobiles. It is said that automobile production on an efficient scale requires an annual output of about 600 000 cars, while in Latin America one-half of this quantity is produced in about 40 plants. The fusion of national markets would have to be accompanied by changes in government policies in Latin America, however, since the proliferation of small car companies has been encouraged by tax and tariff policies followed by the individual countries.

The enlargement of the market through integration would give rise to further gains through the establishment of specialized plants producing parts, components and accessories of automobiles. In the United States, for example, with the expansion of the production of automobiles, components and parts, such as electrical and

100

ignition systems, radiators and heaters, steering wheels, transmissions, and batteries have come to be manufactured in separate plants. Developments in this direction have been observed in Western Europe and, more recently, in Brazil, the largest Latin American country, too. Economic integration promises a continuation of this process, and moves towards the interchangeability of parts and components can bring gains in all countries that have embarked on the production of automobiles.

Further evidence on the importance of the economies of vertical specialization is given in a recent study of the National Industrial Conference Board, that utilized information provided by 147 international companies. According to the findings of this study, material costs are generally lower in U. S. plants than abroad, and the observed differences are explained largely by the low cost of purchased components and fabricated inputs. These intermediate products are supplied by a vast network of specialized producers who enjoy economies of scale on the large U. S. market.[11]

ECONOMIES OF SCALE AND TRANSPORTATION COSTS

In studies on the optimal location of fertilizer and steel plants in Latin America, account has been taken of the cost of transportation as a factor determining the optimum locational pattern. In general, while economies of scale have the effect of enlarging the market area for the products of the individual plant, transportation costs act in the opposite direction. This idea is not new. Around the turn of the century, in a discussion of the location of industry, Alfred Weber suggested that an

[11] Theodore Gates and Fabian Linden, *Costs and Competition*, New York, 1963.

101

optimum locational pattern represents a balance between economies of scale and transportation costs.[12]

In trade among the industrial countries, the relative importance of transportation costs has declined in recent decades, partly as a result of improvements in transportation facilities, and partly in connection with the shift toward the production of commodities with a higher share of value added in the final price. These developments account for the apparent neglect of transportation costs in discussions of economies of scale in a union of industrial countries. Different considerations apply to less developed countries, however.

In an earlier lecture, I made reference to the lack of adequate transportation facilities in the less developed areas of today that will hinder the exploitation of economies of scale after integration. And while transportation costs can be reduced by establishing new, and improving existing facilities, the distance factor will continue to be operative. In this connection, a comparison may be made between population density in Latin America and Africa, on the one hand, and in Western Europe, on the other. With 9 people per square kilometer[13] in Latin America, 7 in Africa, and 86 in Western Europe, the distance factor would appear to restrict the exploitation of economies of scale in the former areas while it is hardly a barrier in Europe.

But population density provides an imperfect indicator of the distance factor for present purposes, since the observed large differences in per capita incomes necessitate the introduction of a weighting procedure. Density is relatively low in the United States, for example, yet, aside from a few industries, such as construction

---

[12] Alfred Weber, *Theory of Location of Industries*, Chicago: University of Chicago Press, 1929, ch. 4.

[13] 1 square kilometer equals 0.3861 square miles. All data refer to the year 1961.

materials, distances do not present an important barrier to obtaining scale economies. On the other hand, population density in Asia is about the same as in Western Europe, but low per capita incomes hinder the exploitation of economies of scale in the latter area. It appears more appropriate, therefore, to calculate the average distance of transporting industrial goods within Western Europe, the United States, and the less developed regions, or, alternatively, to estimate the consumption of manufacturing products per square kilometer.

Among individual industries, the textile and the steel industry can serve as examples. Utilizing data published by the FAO, the consumption of textile products, expressed in terms of fiber content, is calculated as 803 kg per thousand square kilometers in Western Europe, 303 kg in the United States, 39 kg in Latin America, 10 kg in Africa, and 184 kg in Asia. The corresponding figures for steel consumption are 24.57 tons per square kilometer in Western Europe, 9.58 tons in the United States, 0.30 tons in Latin America, 0.13 tons in Africa, and 0.85 tons in Asia.

With the exception of homogeneous products, commodity-by-commodity comparisons are difficult to make, however, and we might instead estimate the density of the consumption of all industrial products taken together or, failing this, that of the gross national product. Using the national income figures referred to before, GNP per square kilometer is calculated as 108.8 thousand dollars for Western Europe, 55.0 thousand dollars for the United States, 3.9 for Latin America, 1.2 for Africa, and 13.4 for Asia.

These comparisons give some indication of the relative importance of the distance-factor, although the figures are subject to several qualifications. From our previous discussion, it follows that GNP per square kilometer data will tend to overestimate the possibilities of exploiting economies of scale by reason of the inclusion of subsistence production in the numerator, and underestimate it by failing to consider prospective increases in national income in a union of less developed countries. The latter comment, although not the former, applies to a comparison of the density of the consumption of individual products, too.

GAINS FROM ECONOMIES OF SCALE

The exploitation of intra-industry economies may involve a replacement or transformation of small scale operations, the substitution of imports from outside the area, or may be associated with increases in consumption. In his "Interregional and International Trade", Bertil Ohlin noted that the first alternative provides one of the sources of gains from international specialization that can be obtained even in the absence of differences in comparative costs. Thus, if countries A and B produce two commodities on a small scale, and at equal costs, both gain from specialization if economies of scale can be appropriated in the two industries.

In discussions on economic integration in less developed areas, however, objections have been raised against the replacement of small firms by larger units and, more generally, against the opening of national markets in the case of existing industries. This position had been taken by some in the course of the Latin America free trade area negotiations, and it has been subsequently endorsed by Sidney Dell. Dell has expressed the view that increased competition in industries established in less developed countries would do more harm than good. For one thing, in an economy characterized by surplus labor, "unless it is plain that the resources employed in an inefficient industry could be readily transferred to better uses, it represents a net loss to the economy to put them out of commission".[14] For another, underdeveloped countries, "having painfully and by great efforts succeeded in establishing a small amount of industry", may not "contemplate with equanimity the opening up of their markets to competition".[15]

This argumentation can be objected to on various grounds. To begin with, industrial skills are generally transferable and therefore the closing down of small scale firms can hardly mean that industrial workers will return to the agricultural "reserve army". Further, by considering only one factor, labor, possible savings attained through the reallocation of capital and entrepreneur are disregarded, although these factors provide important constraints to the economic development of present-day underdeveloped countries.

Neither can we speak about the loss of capital values in small scale firms that are replaced by large scale enterprises since the capital of existing firms represents opportunities foregone. At any rate, the replacement of small scale firms will take time, inasmuch as these will be able to compete as long as their average variable cost is lower than or equal to total cost per unit in the new plants. Finally, in cases when economies of scale entail standardization in the framework of existing firms, there may be no loss of paper values either. In view of our previous discussion, standardization would take place in the textile industry, for example, thereby facilitating the readjustment of individual enterprises.

Let me add that those who oppose trade liberalization for products presently manufactured in the less developed countries generally assume that the growth prospects of these industries are rather poor. Prebisch speaks about

[14] Sidney Dell, *Trade Blocs and Common Markets*, London, Constable, 1963, p. 165.
[15] *Ibid.*

"vegetative growth industries", for example, when referring to the sector of nondurable consumer goods in the Latin American area.

But possibilities for the steady expansion of this sector exist in decades to come. This is indicated by an international comparison of consumption levels in the industry that is usually cited as a prototype of slow-growing sectors —textiles. In 1961, per capita textile fiber consumption was 15.5 kg in the United States, 10.0 kg in the Common Market countries, but only 4.4 kg in Latin America, 2.3 kg in Asia, and 1.8 kg in Africa. At the same time, available evidence indicates that, in less developed areas, the demand for nondurable consumer goods is income-elastic, so that output in these industries can be expected to grow at least in proportion with the rise of national income.

An increase in the demand for nondurable consumer goods will require setting up new factories, and, in the absence of intra-area tariff reductions, the increment in consumption would also be supplied by small scale, inefficient firms. Thus, measures taken to limit competition in consumer goods industries would not only perpetuate the existence of inefficient firms but would also increase their number. At the same time, in several of these industries national monopolies would continue to reap large profits and would be under little pressure to innovate. Finally, the maintenance of protection in industries producing nondurable consumer goods may well lead to demands to restrict competition in the production of durable consumer goods, capital goods, and intermediate products —the so-called dynamic industries.

Turning to the latter industries, we find that as yet, these have been established in few of the less developed countries and hence the replacement of existing firms rarely presents a problem. (The automobile industry in Latin America is an exception.) Correspondingly, the expansion of output would be accompanied by increased consumption and/or a reduction of imports. The former alternative entails a definite gain for the participating countries while the latter can be regarded as "dynamic" trade diversion.

Trade diversion represents a loss for non-participating countries although an expansion in the production of finished manufactures requires increasing imports of machine tools. Further, as the example of continental Europe indicates, at later stages of industrialization an increased exchange of specialized industrial products takes place. In fact, according to the conclusions reached in the previous lecture, the rise in imports accompanying an acceleration of economic growth in less developed areas may ultimately outweigh the trade-diverting effects of integration.

... although an expansion in the exchange
of specialized industrial products ... imports of
manufactures, Europe, at the earlier stages of industrialization, ...
increased exchange of specialized industrial products
takes place. In fact, according to the conclusions reached
in the previous lecture, the rise in imports accompanying an acceleration of economic growth in less
developed areas may ultimately outweigh the
adverse effects of integration.

Chapter V

SOME PROBLEMS OF INTEGRATION IN LESS DEVELOPED AREAS

THE MECHANICS OF TARIFF REDUCTIONS

In the previous lectures I have examined the possible benefits developing countries may derive from their economic integration. In this closing lecture I will discuss several questions that relate to the exploitation and the intra-union distribution of these potential gains. The topics under consideration include changes in internal and external tariffs, the coordination of economic policy, intra-area disparities in the level of development, reciprocity, and payments arrangements.

Regarding the problem of tariff-reductions in an integrated area, note that in the European Common Market, and in the European Free Trade Association, provision has been made for automatic tariff reductions to take place at regular intervals, with the aim of eliminating intra-area tariffs within a specified period. According to the Montevideo Treaty, countries participating in the Latin American Free Trade Area would also have to reduce tariffs by an average of 8 per cent a year and, ultimately, duties on commodities included in the so-called Common List would have to be eliminated. But the actual reduction of tariffs is left to annual item-by-item negotiations, so that it is not known when tariffs on a given commodity will be reduced and, for commodities that are not on the Common List, there is no certainty that tariffs would be removed at all.

At the same time, in the absence of provisions for

111

automatic reductions in duties, the process of tariff reductions shows signs of slowing down in LAFTA. Participating countries generally offered concessions in the first round of negotiations in regard to commodities where tariffs were ineffective anyway but, after the "fat" of protection has been sliced off, further reductions are more difficult to come by. It appears that some countries wish to continue to protect certain industries, while others are reluctant to reduce tariffs because they consider the concessions offered to be inadequate. In view of these developments, it is highly questionable that the original targets could be attained without changing the present rules.

More generally, item-by-item negotiations have the disadvantage of restricting the scope of tariff bargaining and providing room for special interests. At the same time, there is a conflict between the interests of the producer and the user sectors and pressures for protection coming from the side of producers generally prove to be stronger. Finally, the lack of automaticity means that a new decision has to be made to reduce tariffs every year, and changes in the policy of one country can nullify the efforts of others.

On the other hand, across-the-board tariff reductions restrict the influence exerted by special interests and provide for mutual concessions on the part of the contracting parties. The application of an automatic formula also reduces the danger of temporary or permanent interruptions in tariff reductions. Thus, less developed countries are well advised to apply an automatic formula for reducing tariffs in integrating their national economies.

Free Trade Area or Customs Union?

A further question relates to the choice among the various forms of economic integration, such as free trade areas and customs union. Developing countries appear to be inclined to adopt the first alternative —this has indeed happened in LAFTA— in order to maintain their independence in regard to commercial policy. This choice appears to be based on some misapprehensions, however.

Assume, first, that existing restrictions on trade among countries participating in a free trade area are removed irrespective of whether the commodity originates within the area, and that transportation costs are zero. Then, for every commodity, the effective external duty will be that of the country with the lowest tariff since commodities will enter the free trade area wherever they have to pay the smallest duty. In other words, instead of maintaining their independent commercial policy, decisions made by individual countries will be ineffective as long as they do not "undercut" the duties of other member countries. This conclusion will be modified if we introduce transportation costs, but trade deflection will take place as long as tariff differences exceed the additional transportation cost incurred in effecting the transit transaction.

Problems related to the deflection of trade, production, and investment received considerable attention in the course of the European Free Trade Area negotiations. It was argued, for example, that Britain would have an artificial advantage in textile production as she imports grey cloth from Hong Kong duty free and re-exports it in bleached form. To avoid deflection in trade and production, it was then suggested to institute appropriate rules for determining the origin of the commodities traded. A commodity would be regarded as originating within the area if a specified process of transformation takes place in the area or if the value added in the participating countries exceeds a predetermined proportion of the final price. In turn, others expressed

113

the view that while the application of the above rules would reduce trade (and production) deflection, this would not be completely eliminated. In fact, the alleged difficulties of avoiding the deflection of trade and production appear to have played a role in the failure of the negotiations for establishing an all-European free trade area in 1959.

In establishing EFTA, the transformation rule and the requirement that 50 per cent of value added should originate within the area have been adopted. Available information indicates that so far EFTA has not encountered serious problems in the application of these rules. This should not mean, however, that the free trade area form would be appropriate in other instances, too. In this connection, it should be recalled that tariff differences are small among the EFTA countries and, also, the possibilities of trade deflection are limited here by reason of the fact that the participating economies are largely complementary.

Actually, as our previous discussion has indicated, developing countries that participate in regional integration projects are potentially competitive and their tariffs on manufactured goods often differ considerably. With large differences in duties on raw materials, intermediate products, and machinery, the establishment of a free trade area may then entail specialization —and the concomitant establishment of new industries —responding to differences in tariffs rather than to comparative advantages. This will be clear if we consider that the 50 per cent rule has different implications, depending on the tariff levels in the participating countries. Let us assume, for example, that an imported intermediate product accounts for one-third of the final price, while relevant tariff rates are 6 and 2 per cent in EFTA and 60 and 20 per cent in a union of developing countries. Relative differences in duties are the same in both instances, yet in view of the disparities in absolute tariff levels, the country with the lower tariff has an approximately 1 per cent cost-advantage in the first case and 10 per cent in the second.

A further consideration is that, in the presence of large differences in tariff levels, the preferences accorded to partner countries will differ depending on the level of external tariffs. Take the case, for example, when the average tariff level is 20 per cent in country A and 45 per cent in country B. After the elimination of intra-area duties, A would thus give a 20 per cent preference to B and receive a 45 per cent preference in return. At the same time, by manipulating tariffs on the products of individual industries, countries can ensure differential advantages for themselves and can also reduce the value of concessions given. Should one also consider the administrative problems involved in policing trade and production deflection, it would appear desirable that developing countries aimed at establishing a customs union rather than a free trade area.

PROTECTION IN A UNION OF LESS DEVELOPED COUNTRIES

The question arises, then, how the common tariff of a customs union of developing countries should be set. In general, a common tariff lower than the average of the duties of individual countries can have the same protective effect by reason of the trade diverting effects of a customs union and the lowering of costs due to large scale economies. Still, the question, remains, as to the "appropriate" height and structure of the common tariff.

As a general rule, one may say the common tariff should be set so as to serve the objective of accelerating the rate of economic growth with the maintenance of

115

permissible levels of balance-of-payments equilibrium. But the attainment of this objective requires establishing realistic exchange rates along with the setting of tariffs. I have previously noted that overvalued exchange rates in many underdeveloped countries have discriminated against export activities. The establishment of realistic exchange rates would, then, contribute to the expansion of exports to third countries.

Export activities would be further helped by the process of economic transformation in a union of developing countries. In view of our previous discussion, the appropriation of internal and external economies can lead to lower costs in the union, and greater competition will have the same effect. Correspondingly, the comparative advantage of these countries may also change. In general, in industries where large scale economies play an important role, comparative advantage is largely the result of historical developments, including the extension of domestic markets. Developing countries are likely first to become competitive in labor-intensive industries or in industries based on domestic materials. In much of the manufacturing industry, however, external economies are of importance, and hence competitiveness presupposes a parallel advance along a broad front. At the same time, such developments take time by reason of the amount of capital and skills required and are not likely to occur without some degree of protection.

The question arises, then, whether a union of developing countries should use selective duties to protect certain industries or should apply the same tariff to all products. Selective tariffs have been advocated in connection with the infant industry argument. One may rightly ask the question, however, whether governments necessarily choose the "right" industries and whether they may not come under the influence of special interests in making the selection.

As an alternative solution, it has been suggested to apply a general tariff of identical rates to all industries so as to avoid interference with the market mechanism within the industrial sector. But would we escape arbitrariness in setting a general tariff? This would be true only in a rather special case. It is easy to see that a general tariff would provide equal treatment to all protected commodities in the event that tariffs applied solely to final goods, while raw materials, intermediate products, and machinery entered duty free. In the presence of duties on various inputs, however, a general tariff would not be "neutral" and its effects would depend on the relative importance of interindustry relationships in various branches of manufacturing.

Nevertheless, while we have to reject the proposal to apply a general tariff to all industries, the idea of neutrality is worth exploring. I wish to suggest here that in a union of developing countries efforts should be made to establish neutral tariffs on manufactured goods in the sense that no industries be given artificial advantage through protection. The objective of neutrality, if correctly interpreted, also requires taking account of differences in social and private productivity by correcting the effects of external economies.

It appears, then, that the common tariff of a union of developing countries should not be established as an average of national tariffs, but rather two separate decisions need to be made. The first decision concerns the choice of the average tariff level on manufactured goods with a view to the objective of accelerating the rate of economic growth in the union; the second relates to the structure of tariffs when the criterion of neutrality should be applied, with appropriate adjustments made for differences in social and private productivity.

It appears, then, that the determination of common tariffs in a union is not a simple matter but requires careful deliberation on the part of the governments of the participating countries. This presupposes a coordination of commercial policy and, to some extent, of development policies. The question arises, then, what degree of policy coordination would be necessary in a union of developing countries.

While the basic objective of these countries is to accelerate their economic growth, in the process of development it is necessary to avoid duplication of production facilities and to ensure adequate specialization. Classical economic theory tells us that these goals can be attained by relying on the price mechanism, which, indeed, appears to serve this function reasonably well in present-day industrial countries. Government interference with the price mechanism is limited in countries such as the United States and Germany, although it is somewhat more pronounced in France. In the latter case, the government exerts influence on private investment decisions through the publication of targets, moral suasion, and by the granting of investment credit.

The price system fulfills its allocative function less satisfactorily in underdeveloped areas, where capital and labor markets are often fragmented and differences between social and private profitability may be considerable. Correspondingly, government intervention will have greater scope here and some degree of planning appears desirable. Governments may prepare guidelines as in the French system of planning, for example, although formulated according to the needs of the developing countries. Appropriate provisions should also be made for economic and social overhead capital. Government intervention may be necessary in monopolistic industries and, last but not least, measures need to be taken to coordinate the activities of governmental and semi-governmental agencies that is often found wanting in less developed countries.

Now, if we accept the premise that some form of development planning is desirable in the less developed countries, there will also be need for a certain degree of coordination of these plans in a union in order to avoid possible conflicts. This is not to say that the establishment of a supranational planning authority would be a necessity; in the absence of political unity, this does not appear to be realistic anyway. One may rather envisage a confrontation of national plans to avoid overlapping in investment decisions and to create transparency with respect to cost conditions and demand prospects. These objectives would be served by locational studies and by long-term projections. Locational studies may be helpful in comparing the possibilities of establishing pulp and paper mills in Mexico, Brazil, and Chile, while long-term forecasts can provide guidance for the future expansion of national industries.

And how about agreements on specialization? Should goverments enter into bargaining regarding the establishment of new industries? I think that we can hardly expect government bargaining to lead to a desirable locational structure; rather, it would appear preferable to leave this to the forces of competition except in cases where large capital requirements will not permit private financing. In the latter instances, an autonomous development bank can serve an important role. A bank of this type can be set up from subscriptions by the member governments and may be empowered to issue bonds on international money markets.

Lending itself should be made to depend on objective criteria; it would appear desirable that the bank relied on detailed locational and cost studies in granting cre-

119

dit. At the same time, the effectiveness of foreign aid could be increased by channeling it through the bank instead of continuing the present system of distribution. Finally, the proposed investment bank could also have the function of guaranteeing private loans extended to the industries of the area.

THE PROBLEM OF RECIPROCITY

In discussions on economic integration in less developed areas in general, and in Latin America in particular, frequent references have been made to the need for reciprocity among the participating countries. There is no general agreement, however, as to what is meant by "reciprocity", and hence, in order to evaluate these claims, we have to survey the various definitions in use.

It has been suggested that reciprocity be understood to mean equilibrium in intra-area trade for each country; i. e., none of the participating countries are to export more to the other member countries of the area than what they import. This emphasis on equilibrium in intra-area trade appears to be misdirected, however, since it puts an additional constraint on the flow of international trade. As long as each nation's balance-of-payments with all other countries, taken together, is in equilibrium, it matters little whether they have a surplus or a deficit in intra-area trade. Thus, a mineral producer may continue to run a surplus with non-member countries, and a deficit in intra-area trade, without the need for corrective measures.

Actually, measures taken to balance intra-area trade would create disequilibrium in the total balance-of-payments of individual countries which, in turn, would necessitate the application of further corrective measures. Ultimately, trade might well diminish, inasmuch as these measures are likely to take the form of restrictions on the part of countries incurring a deficit rather than concessions by countries that show a surplus.

Another concept of reciprocity that has gained currency since the signing of the Montevideo Treaty would require a parallel expansion of intra-area trade to result from the mutual concessions given by the contracting parties. This principle thus calls for the equilibrium of the *increment* in trade among the member countries of the union through an appropriate balancing of tariff concessions. Its application is open to several objections, however.

To begin with, an expansion of intra-area trade following the establishment of a union cannot be attributed solely to reductions in tariffs; it may also be due to intercountry differences in competitiveness, inflationary pressures, or an over and undervaluation of exchange rates. In order to ensure the equality of increases in the intra-area exports and imports of each country, it would be necessary, therefore, that changes in intra-area trade due to the operation of the latter factors be counterbalanced by disparities in the concessions offered. This can hardly be considered a proper objective, however, since it would reward countries with overvalued exchange rates and inflationary policies and penalize others.

At any rate, inequalities in the absolute increase of intra-area trade may be necessary to re-establish equilibrium in the balance-of-payments of surplus or deficit countries. Further, even if all participating countries were initially in balance-of-payments equilibrium, the maintenance of equilibrium may require imbalances in the expansion of intra-area exchange. This conclusion follows, since integration will affect the intra-area and the extra-area trade of the participating countries in differing degrees, and these changes should again be

121

considered jointly rather than in isolation. To give an example, an expansion of the exports of manufactured goods from a member country to other countries of the area may be accompanied by increased imports of raw materials and foodstuffs from outside the area.

It appears, then, that neither equilibrium in intra-area trade nor a balancing of the increment of this trade can be regarded as an appropriate objective. Alternatively, it has been suggested that reciprocity should mean an even distribution of industry throughout the integrated area. This proposition gives expression to a judgment concerning the superiority of industry over agriculture and it also calls for dispensing with locational considerations in the establishment of new factories. Accordingly, one could propose, for example, that the grain producing areas of the United States should industrialize without regard to the economic costs of such a change. This would hardly be considered desirable, and an unqualified espousal of the principle of an even distribution of industry is likely to slow down rather than accelerate economic growth in an integrated area.

Instead, I propose to define reciprocity as an equality of opportunity, that would involve dispensing with artificial measures which would give advantage to one country or another, and would also entail correcting for "polarization" tendencies. This interpretation of the principle of reciprocity leads us, then, to a consideration of the problem of intra-area disparities in opportunities for economic growth.

INTERREGIONAL DISPARITIES IN LESS DEVELOPED AREAS

You will recall that while, according to the classical theory, the free play of competitive forces would eliminate interregional income differences, in recent times several writers have argued that without government intervention these interregional disparities may increase rather than decline. According to Myrdal, the outcome will be determined by "spread" and "backwash" effects emanating from the more developed regions, when the former include increased demand for the products of less developed regions and the transmission of technological knowledge, and the latter refer to the movement of capital and skilled labor from underdeveloped to developed regions, and to changes in the locational pattern of industries to the detriment of the backward regions.

Now, in industrial countries, the spread-effects appear to dominate, inasmuch as a highly developed price system permits the exploitation of cost differences and the existence of transportation and communication facilities contributes to interregional exchange. We find, for example, that interregional disparities in incomes have been declining in the United States, and while in Western Europe inequalities between the North and the South create serious problems for Italy, the disparities issue is of comparatively little importance in the more developed countries, such as Germany and the United Kingdom.

The backwash-effects play a greater role in underdeveloped areas, however. With an imperfect price system, primitive transportation facilities, and an uneven distribution of social and economic overhead in these areas, agglomerative tendencies assume importance. These are related to the availability of overhead capital, skilled labor and linked industrial processes, when the latter not only provide ready markets and low-cost inputs but also contribute to future improvements through the exchange of technological information and induced technical change.

At the same time, the less favored regions can be said

123

to be financing the industrial development of their more advanced counterparts by paying higher than world-market prices for industrial products in intra-area trade. By comparison, backward regions may derive little benefit from integration if they continue to supply primary products at pre-union prices. The balance of advantages will further be affected by the distribution of tariff revenues which appears to have favored the more advanced Kenya at the expense of Uganda and Tanganyika in the East African Customs Territory.

In turn, one may argue that the industrial development of particular regions would benefit others through increased demand for their products that allows for improvements in production methods, and may also permit the establishment of processing facilities. In evaluating the importance of these spill-over effects, one should not lose sight of the supply side, however —namely the supply of capital needed for improving production processes and establishing processing plants. The supply of savings in less developed areas being limited, new capital may have the tendency to move to regions favored by agglomeration economies.

In addition, in cases where the less developed regions have some manufacturing industry, these industries might suffer from the liberalization of intra-area trade. This result has been observed after the unification of Italy, for example. The political and economic integration of Italy in the second half of the nineteenth century led to an outflow of capital and setbacks to indigenous industry in Southern Italy, and thereby contributed to a retardation of improvements in living standards in the latter area.

The danger of polarization in a union of developing countries is related to the degree of economic development in the constituent regions. This problem is of special importance in Latin America, where the industries of Mexico and Brazil are relatively developed while Bolivia or Paraguay are far behind in the process of industrialization. Existing industries in the former countries are likely to attract further industries and the latter may lose some of their manufacturing facilities.

By comparison, most African countries have little to lose since they start out by and large on an equal footing. But exceptions can be found also here, as indicated by the case of the East African Federation, where new manufacturing industries were located chiefly around Nairobi and Mombassa, partly in response to the existence of sea ports, and partly by reason of the benefits provided by the availability of related industries. Correspondingly, as noted in the report of the Raisman Commission between the years 1952-54 and 1957-59, per capita incomes in Kenya increased by about 40 per cent, in Tanganyika by less than 20 per cent, and in Uganda little, if at all. Similar conclusions have been reached in regard to the Federation of Rhodesia and Nyasaland where mining operations provided the center of attraction.

Within a national economy, the problem of interregional disparities can be handled by appropriate governmental policies but, in a union of less developed countries, the situation is aggravated by reason of the existence of independent decision making bodies. To counteract the polarization tendencies, a coordination of the regional policies undertaken by the national governments of the member countries is therefore necessary. This would involve a common understanding in the formulation of objectives as well as a coordination of the measures to be taken. The latter may include the lengthening of the transitional period for the countries at a lower level of economic development, the establishment of overhead facilities, investment bank loans, and a variety of fiscal measures.

125

In discussions of economic integration in less developed areas, interest has recently been focused on payments arrangements. The experience of the European Payments Union is often recalled and it is claimed that the establishment of an intra-area payments system is a precondition of increased trade among the member countries of a union. On the other hand, the opponents of such schemes maintain that the experience of the EPU is not relevant for a union of developing countries, since trade-relations among the latter are much less extensive than in Europe, and, at any rate, with the advent of convertibility, the EPU itself has been dissolved. It is further argued that —at least in Latin America and in Africa— the currencies of the majority of the developing countries are convertible, and hence a payments union would represent a backward step.

Correspondingly, in a discussion of payments arrangements for a union of less developed areas, distinction should first be made according to whether convertible currencies predominate in the area. The case of inconvertible currencies, characteristic of much of Southeast Asia, does not have to detain us long. A payments union appears to be a useful device here, and can indeed lead to an expansion of intra-area trade. In fact, the example of the EPU indicates that establishing a payments union may ultimately contribute to convertibility.

But some kind of payments arrangement can prove to be useful even in less developed areas where the majority of the currencies are convertible since the scarcity of foreign exchange impinge on international trade here, too. In Latin America, for example, in addition to tariffs, trade is restricted by the use of various devices, such as pre-payment requirements and differential taxes, all of which increase the cost of importation.

Convertibility is thus often maintained through the employment of measures that represent a "cross" between tariffs and exchange control.

Accordingly, the liberalization of intra-area trade has to be accompanied by the abolition of these measures, and the establishment of a payments union may ease the attendant balance-of-payments difficulties. Payments agreements could further contribute to the financing of the increase in trade among the member-countries of the integrated area.

If we accept the premise that payments arrangements are desirable in a union of less developed countries, we face the further question as to what form these arrangements should take. In discussions centering around LAFTA, several proposals have been made, two of which have attracted widespread attention: ECLA's scheme for a EPU-type agency and Robert Triffin's plan for a Latin American clearing house.

ECLA proposes the establishment of an international agency that would operate as a clearing-mechanism and would also provide automatic credits within prescribed limits to finance deficits arising in intra-area trade. ECLA's plan thus relies on the original interpretation of the reciprocity principle, according to which the intra-area trade of each participating country should be balanced. I have noted the objections against this principle, and these do not need to be repeated. I may now add that under ECLA's plan debtor countries would be encouraged to use their export receipts originating outside the area to increase their extra-area imports or to build up exchange reserves, while taking advantage of intra-area credit facilities. On the other hand, creditor countries would find their intra-area export earnings "locked in" and their response may well be a reduction of intra-area exports rather than an increase in imports.

In turn, Triffin proposed the establishment of a clearing house as the first step, to be followed by the granting of reciprocal credits on a modest scale based on the overall rather than the intra-area balance-of-payments position of the member countries. This plan removes the principal deficiencies of the ECLA proposal, although it would run into difficulties if all —or most— countries of an area were to incur a balance-of-payments deficit. In such a situation, an incentive would be provided to use up credit margins at an early date.

It appears, then, that a payments arrangement that provided credits on the basis of the overall balance-of-payments position of the participating countries also presupposes an equilibrium in the balance-of-payments of the union. Excessive inflation or deflation in some of the participating countries could thus play havoc with such a scheme and, in fact, in the discussions on payments arrangements the maintenance of fixed exchange rates and the absence of disparities in monetary policies appears to have been taken for granted.

This assumption may indeed be made in regard to African countries that belong to the sterling or to the franc areas. The history of Latin American republics presents a rather different picture, however, and it can hardly be assumed that these countries would fall in step in regard to their monetary policies in the future. At the same time, it appears questionable that they would accept a coordination of monetary policies as proposed by Javier Márquez, which would be necessary for maintaining fixed exchange rates.

But, should fixed exchange rates necessarily be regarded as an objective? In my work *The Theory of Economic Integration* I have argued that fixed rates are indeed desirable for a union of industrial countries, although some flexibility in the rates may be called for during the transitional period. On the other hand, many of the arguments favoring fixed rates in a common market of advanced industrial countries have little relevance for a union of less developed economies. In the absence of a well-developed foreign exchange market, the danger of speculation in short-term funds is limited while long-term funds could be denominated in some international unit. An international unit (the Latin dollar?) could also be used in commercial contracts —as it has indeed been done by utilizing the U. S. dollar for this purpose.

A further consideration is that while existing parities might be taken as equilibrium rates in most European countries, and structural changes due to integration might require little adjustment in these rates, this can hardly be said as regards Latin American currencies. In fact, as I have noted before, the value of these currencies is maintained through the combined application of high tariffs, prepayment requirements, and similar devices, and a liberalization of trade would necessitate adjustments in the exchange rates. And even if these parities were equilibrium rates in the present situation, the structural changes attendant upon development *cum* integration could hardly fail to affect them. Correspondingly, in a system of fixed exchange rates, the reallocation of resources may well take place at the wrong rates.

These arguments would point to the need to give appropriate consideration to the possibility of the introduction of flexible rates for LAFTA —an alternative which has received no mention in the discussions. Flexible rates do not necessarily mean freely floating rates, however, and it may appear desirable to set up an Exchange Equalization Fund for LAFTA with the purpose of avoiding excessive fluctuations in parities. Finally, flexible rates do not have to be adopted for an indefinite period but, with the development of the participating economies and the acceptance of the idea of monetary coordination, a return to fixed rates can be effected.

129

The adoption of a system of flexible exchange rates would reduce the need for international liquidity which underlies the various schemes for payments agreements. At the same time, a system of export credits (denominated in some international unit) and export insurance, as well as the establishment of correspondent relations among Latin American banks, can provide assistance to the expansion of trade.

APPENDIX

DYNAMIC EXTERNAL ECONOMIES
AND MARKET SIZE

THE CONCEPT AND CLASSIFICATION OF EXTERNAL ECONOMIES

It is often claimed that the introduction of the concept of external economies by Marshall was meant to rescue long-run competitive equilibrium in the presence of increasing returns.[1] A rereading of the *Principles* suggests, however, that Marshall did not share the excessive preoccupation of his followers with competitive equilibrium. Marshall was aware of the fact that "economic problems are imperfectly presented when they are treated as problems of statical equilibrium, and not of... growth",[2] and —although he was far from presenting a complete theory of growth— his valuable insights into the interrelationship of external economies and economic progress foreshadowed later, modern treatment.

Marshallian external economies are not the bucolic ones of the bee-orchard-honey type,[3] but are all closely connected with the development of the economy. They are said to depend on "the general development of industry", on "the growth of correlated branches of industry", on "the general progress of industrial environ-

---

[1] On this point, cf. F. M. Bator, "The Anatomy of Market Failure", *Quarterly Journal of Economics*, August, 1958, p. 356.

[2] *Principles of Economics*, p. 382.

[3] J. E. Meade's famous example of direct interaction between producers, when the beekeeper's bees enjoy the free food provided by the applegrower's orchard blossoms.

ment", and on the increase of the size of the market in general.[4] External economies include "the many various economies of specialized skill and specialized machinery, of localized industries and production on a large scale", the "increased facilities of communication of all kinds", trade knowledge, skilled labor force, etc.[5] The pervading theme in the discussion of external economies is their interaction with the growth of the economy. Marshall also points out that many of these economies are irreversible, so that the gains due to increased production are not lost if output returns to its former level.[6]

Since Marshall's time the concept of external economies has received varied treatment. Some authors, like Frank H. Knight, tend to dismiss external economies altogether;[7] others have attempted to classify and reclassify them in a static framework.[8] The dynamic interpretation of external economies is of recent origin.[9] In this study, external economies will be defined as a

[4] *Principles*, pp. 221, 264, 267-68, 365.

[5] *Ibid.*, pp. 237, 267, 365-66.

[6] *Ibid.*, Appendix H.

[7] "Some Fallacies in the Interpretation of Social Cost", *Readings in Price Theory*, Chicago, Richard D. Irwin, 1952, pp. 160-79.

[8] Jacob Viner, "Cost Curves and Supply Curves", *ibid.*, pp. 198-232; J. E. Meade, "External Economies and Diseconomies in a Competitive Situation", *Economic Journal*, March, 1952, pp. 54-67; M. C. Kemp, "The Efficiency of Competition as an Allocator of Resources, I. External Economies in Production", *Canadian Journal of Economics and Political Science*, February, 1955, pp. 30-42; F. M. Bator, *op. cit.*, pp. 351-79.

[9] Cf., e. g., Paul Rosenstein-Rodan, "Problems of Industrialization of Eastern and South-Eastern Europe", *Economic Journal*, June-September, 1943, pp. 202-11; Tibor Scitovsky, "Two Concepts of External Economies", *Journal of Political Economy*, April, 1954, pp. 143-51; Marcus Fleming, "External Economies and the Doctrine of Balanced Growth", *Economic Journal*, June, 1955, pp. 241-56; Ragnar Nurkse, *Problems of Capital Formation in Underdeveloped Countries*, Oxford: Basil Blackwell, 1953; Arthur Lewis, *The Theory of Economic Growth*, Chicago, Richard D. Irwin, 1955; Albert Hirschman, *The Strategy of Economic Development*, New Haven: Yale University Press, 1958.

divergence between social and private product, when social and private products are interpreted as the present value of future (direct and indirect) benefits. This definition includes both static and dynamic external economies in production, but excludes external effects in consumption.

In regard to external economies as defined here, we shall first distinguish between economies operating outside of the market mechanism and those working through the market.[10] As a further subdivision within the first group, we also differentiate between static economies and those operating through time. This three-fold classification will prove to be useful in examining the interrelationship of external economies and growth.[11]

The time-element is absent from the static external economies, which are the only kind compatible with static equilibrium. Direct interaction between producers, the use of a common pool of resources, and Meade's concept of the creation of "atmosphere"[12] belong to this category. The first form of static economies can be represented by the bee-orchard example; the second prevails if fishermen or oil-drillers use a common pool of fish or oil; the third is typified by increased rainfall due to afforestation. In the first two instances, the quantity of the unpaid resource decreases by its use, while it remains unchanged in the third case. Never-

[10] No explicit distinction will be made between economies that are external to the firm and internal to the industry, and inter-industry economies. Nevertheless, it can be said that, by and large, non-market interactions correspond to the former, and market interactions to the latter.

[11] A fourth kind of external economy: the impact of market size on specialization, will be considered separately, since this refers to changes in the *structure* of industries, rather than to the interrelationship of *existing* industries.

[12] Atmosphere is defined by Meade as a fixed condition of production which is unchanged in quantity irrespective of use. *Trade and Welfare*, p. 41.

theless, the use of "atmosphere" is also limited by the number of producers who have access to it. In the celebrated example of afforestation, for instance, only the farmers of a certain region benefit. Static external economies are favored examples in textbooks, but have little importance in the real world and will not be discussed here.

The second category of external economies operates through time and outside of the market mechanism. It comprises the spreading of technological and organizational know-how and the development of a managerial class and a skilled labor force. One could argue that, at any given point of time, the acquisition of techniques and the hiring of labor takes place from a "pool" of knowledge and skilled personnel (the former is analogous to Meade's atmosphere, the latter to the pool of oil and fish), so that the existence of this type of external economies is consistent with static general equilibrium, *if* technological knowledge and skills are considered as given. However, firms do not solely enjoy existing technical knowledge and skills, but also constantly create and develop them. The non-market interaction of firms in this field consists not only in the sharing and using of existing technical know-how, but technology also "begets" new technology, and contributes to further development. Putting it in a different way, technology and skills are developed through use. We face a dynamic process in the growth and acquisition of skills, and technological and organizational knowledge, hence —for the discussion of problems of economic growth— the static interpretation of this category of external economies would be of little use.[13]

[13] The creation of social overhead capital comprising educational and hygienic facilities necessary for developing a labor force that will possess the required qualities also belongs to this category. This relationship is not in one direction, however. As H. W. Singer rightly points out, industrial development also

The third category of external economies is also a phenomenon of dynamic change but, unlike the second, it operates through the market mechanism. These pecuniary economies include market interactions between industries that entail a divergence between private profitability and social productivity. Pecuniary external economies have no relevance for static equilibrium: in static theory prices (and output) are considered as resulting from a given market situation, and we do not inquire into the historical process of how these prices have come about. They are of importance, however, under conditions of dynamic change since they affect the growth of the economy. This warrants a more detail ed discussion of external economies operating through the market.

PECUNIARY EXTERNAL ECONOMIES

Pecuniary economies have been defined above as inter-industry relationships operating through the market mechanism that entail a divergence between social productivity, and private profitability. These interrelationships may take the form of direct market interactions or may operate via income changes. In the first case, industries are interconnected as buyers and suppliers of raw material and intermediate products, in the second, as suppliers of consumer goods. We will first examine the direct market interactions of producers and discuss interdependence via changes in incomes at a later point.

The direct interdependence of industries on the market

reacts "on the general level of education, skill, way of life, inventiveness, habits, store of technology, creation of new demand, etc." ("The Distribution of Gains between Investing and Borrowing Countries", *American Economic Review*, Papers and Proceedings, May, 1950, p. 476.)

can be analyzed under varying assumptions.[14] We may assume that positive net investment takes place, and

 (a) factor supplies are inelastic and there are no internal economies;
 (b) factor supplies are elastic, but internal economies are absent;
 (c) there are economies internal to the firm or to the industry, while factor supplies may be elastic or inelastic.

In all these cases, two types of market interactions will be distinguished: the impact of an expansion in industry A on output-using industry B and on input-producing industry C.[15] The expansion of industry A, in turn, might have been prompted by an increase in the demand for its product, or by the introduction of an innovation. An increase in demand for the commodity manufactured by industry A will raise the demand for the product of input-producing industry C, while an innovation in A will reduce the price of its product that is used as an input in industry B. At the same time, if the innovation is output-increasing and input-using,[16]

[14] The reader will note that differences in the assumptions made by Rosenstein-Rodan, Nurkse, Scitovsky, Fleming, etc., are largely responsible for divergences in the views expressed by these authors on the subject of external economies.

[15] Further types of market interactions between industries are mentioned by Scitovsky ("Two Concepts of External Economies", *op. cit.*, p. 49): industry A's products may be complementary to those of industry D; and the factors used by industry A may have substitutes in industry E's products. In addition, external diseconomies are generated in industry F, the products of which are substitutes of those of industry A and in industry C, whose products are complementary (in other uses) to the factors used by industry A. These secondary repercussions will not be discussed here, although this does not amount to the denial of their importance.

[16] See the classification of innovations given in Oscar Lange, "A Note on Innovations", *Readings in the Theory of Income Distribution*, Philadelphia: Blakiston, 1946, pp. 181-96.

demand for $C's$ products will also increase. The effects of an innovation of the latter type will be examined below.

In case (a),[17] if an innovation takes place in industry A, the price of the products manufactured in industries A and B will fall, and their production, as well as output in input-producing industry C, will expand. Nevertheless —factor supplies being inelastic— prices of other commodities will rise. The real effect of the innovation on the national product will be equivalent to the output produced with the inputs saved in industry A at its original production level, to which its possible impact on the allocation of investment funds should be added.

Under the assumption of perfect foresight, investment decisions in all industries will be guided by correct anticipations of future demands and relative prices, and private profitability and social productivity considerations will coincide. Removing the assumption of perfect foresight, these decisions will be based on present prices which only imperfectly reflect future scarcities. In the absence of information on the expansion of industry A, less than the efficient amount will be invested in industries B and C, and —without the corresponding developments in the buyer and supplier industries— investment in A will also be less than desired. Thus, from a given amount of investment funds available in the economy, more will be spent in other fields than would be considered desirable. This is equivalent to saying that the private profitability of an investment in industry A understates its social productivity.

Our results will be modified under case (b), where it is assumed that at least some of the factors of production are available in elastic supply. This is the case

[17] This case is discussed in Scitovsky's article.

discussed by Rosenstein-Rodan, Lewis, and Nurkse. The first two of these authors assume an elastic labor supply, Professor Nurkse an elastic supply of capital. If the high elasticity of the labor-supply is interpreted as involuntary unemployment, and the elastic supply of capital means that, in the absence of a minimum rate of earnings, capital would be used for improductive purposes, the expansion in industries B and C represents a real gain for the economy. In other words, if the supplier and buyer industries can utilize hitherto unused resources,[18] the innovation raises national product through (a) its input-saving effect in industry A, and (b) its impact on the expansion in interdependent industries. Now the private profitability of industry A will not only understate its social utility but it is also possible that the government will have to undertake an unprofitable investment in A in order to ensure the desired expansion in the interrelated industries.[19]

Under more general assumptions, in case (c), an innovation in industry A gives the possibility of obtaining economies of scale in some of the industries involved. Supply industries will be able to use large scale production methods as their output increases, while at succeeding stages of production the lowering of input-prices can have a similar effect. In other words, a successful innovation in an industry producing intermediate goods will induce suppliers and buyers to reconsider their production methods and to employ hitherto

[18] Besides labor and capital, these considerations apply also to unutilized water-power and mineral supplies, provided that the latter cannot be economically transported for export purposes.

[19] This kind of pecuniary external economy assumes an eminent place in most writings on economic development. It is often pointed out that in underdeveloped countries the creation of economic overhead (transportation facilities, electricity, water, gas, sewage, etc.) will make the expansion of manufacturing industries possible.

140

not used advanced technology. The newly applied technology might have been known to the entrepreneur before, it may represent new application of existing scientific knowledge, or may be associated with new developments through research.

The transmission of technological change may also take the form of a circular process. In England around 1800, for example, a circular flow ran from iron making to steam engines to coal mining and to iron making again. Under such a configuration, technological improvements have a magnified impact, since increased productivity in one industry reverts to it in the form of cheaper inputs. All these repercussions —vertical or triangular— form part of a response mechanism that contributes to the development of technology as the economy grows. In a given stage of expansion, further gains are forthcoming if elastic factor-supplies restrain increases in the prices of productive factors.

The above considerations focus attention on the interdependence of industries. All industries are sources and recipients of external economies; thus the concept should not be limited to the impact of the provision of economic overhead on other industries, but should include the effects and inter-effects of an expansion in any industry. As Rosenstein-Rodan expressed it, "complementarity makes to some extent all industries basic".[20] But Rosenstein-Rodan neglected to add that industries, in addition to being complementary, are also competitive in their demand for resources.

Emphasis on complementary relationships at the expense of competitive interrelations between industries led Rosenstein-Rodan and Nurkse to concentrate their attention on external economies operating via income changes. Under this conception, the installation of ef-

[20] "Problems of Industrialization of Eastern and South-Eastern Europe", op. cit., p. 208.

141

ficient large-scale plants in the production of certain consumer goods would generate demand for other items of consumption by raising real income, but the introduction of large scale technology is checked by the limited size of the market in underdeveloped countries. According to these authors, the economies of scale referred to here could be captured, if an increase in incomes was achieved as a result of the joint installation of plants of efficient size in a number of industries. However, as Marcus Flaming noted, "so long as factors of production are in fixed supply, the introduction of large scale production units is likely to give rise not to economies but to diseconomies in other industries unless the former industries are already big enough for the introduction of the new plant to make possible a net reduction in the resources employed there".[21] Beneficial effects through income-changes will nevertheless occur if the supply of resources is elastic, or if internal or external economies have already raised national income and the resulting increased demand has made possible the introduction of efficient large scale production methods in some industries.

MARKET SIZE AND EXTERNAL ECONOMIES

It is now generally realized that inter-industry relationships play a significant role in the process of economic growth. The importance of "linkages" between various industries was first noted by Schumpeter who directed attention to the impact of the emergence of new industries on the growth of a national economy.[22] Recently, François Perroux examined the role of an *indus-*

[21] "External Economies and the Doctrine of Balanced Growth", *Economic Journal*, June, 1955, p. 247.
[22] "The Instability of Capitalism", *Economic Journal*, September, 1928, pp. 361-86.

trie motrice in economic development. Perroux expounds that a growing industry creates external economies for supplier and user industries, and these industries together with the *industrie motrice* form a "pole of development", which, in turn, contributes to the growth of the economy.[23] Arguing along similar lines, Professor Hirschman advises underdeveloped countries to establish industries producing intermediate products where the combined amount of the backward and forward linkage effects is the largest.[24]

These explanations lay great stress on how a key industry affects the development of the linked industries, but fail to specify the *conditions* of the fulfillment which is necessary for the key industry to expand. Concerning these conditions, economic historians have paid ample attention to the side of supply, but only recently has there been more consideration given to demand factors.[25] This long-time neglect of demand factors is far from justified, however. The availability of materials is not sufficient to warrant the development of an industry as long as satisfactory outlets are not found

[23] "Note sur la notion de 'pôle de croissance'", *Economie Appliquée*, January-June, 1955, pp. 309-20. For a similar formulation, cf. H. W. Singer, "The Distribution of Gains between Investing and Borrowing Countries", *American Economic Review*, Papers and Proceedings, May, 1950, pp. 473-85.

[24] *The Strategy of Economic Development*, Ch. 6. The concept of backward and forward linkages refers to quantitative relationships between interdependent industries that are derived from an input-output table. Note that the assumption of constant technological coefficients excludes the consideration of changes in costs.

[25] E. W. Gilboy notes that "in the field of economic history as well as that of economic theory there has been a tendency to overemphasize the factor of supply". ("Demand as a Factor in the Industrial Revolution", in *Facts and Factors in Economic History*, Cambridge: Harvard University Press, 1932, p. 620.) This charge cannot be levied against German historians. See, for example, Werner Sombart's *Luxus und Kapitalismus* and *Krieg und Kapitalismus*.

for its product. The market for industrial expansion might become available at home, as a result of an increase in per capita incomes and population, the introduction of new wants, military demand, or demand for further transformation in production, or abroad, in the form of possibilities for exportation.[26]

Historical experience gives evidence of the restrictive effects of limited markets on the expansion of various industries as well as of manufacturing industry in general. It is noted e. g., that, notwithstanding the early cost-reducing innovations in weaving and spinning, the development of the British textile industry did not accelerate until the domestic market sufficiently expanded and large scale sales on foreign markets became profitable. The breakthrough in the textile industry, in turn, provided a stimulus for the iron industry via the demand for steam engines and textile machinery.[27] The availability of export markets was instrumental in the expansion of other British manufacturing industries, too.

Export possibilities were of prime importance also in the industrial development of the continental countries. The expansion of the German metallurgical and engineering industries, for example, would not have been possible without foreign markets. Military expenditures and, in its initial stage, railroad building, too, influenced industrialization through demand for the products of heavy industry. This line of thought can be

[26] Among these factors, consumer demand is singled out by Hobson, who formulates one of the preconditions of capitalistic development in his *Evolution of Modern Capitalism* as "the existence of large, accessible markets with populations willing and economically able to consume the products of capitalist industry".

[27] Cf., e. g., Goran Ohlin, "Balanced Economic Growth in History", *American Economic Review*, Papers and Proceedings, May, 1959, pp. 345-49.

conveniently summed up in referring to Goran Ohlin's conclusion, according to which "the first step towards... an understanding of the growth process is simply to pay as much attention to the growth of an industry's market as is usually lavished on the growth of its capacity".[28]

The evidence cited above indicates that exports had been one of the main forms of market outlets for the advanced economies of today during their period of industrial development.[29] On the other hand, for present-day underdeveloped countries, tariffs and other forms of trade barriers, payments restrictions, divergences in economic policies and political uncertainty constitute serious obstacles in the way of basing the expansion of manufacturing industries on export possibilities. At the same time, the domestic market seldom provides sufficient outlet either. A comparison of recent experience in Puerto Rico and in Chile can serve to illustrate this point. Although the Chilean economy possesses considerable natural advantages over Puerto Rico, the record of the latter has been far more favorable. This result could not have been obtained had the Puerto Rican economy not possessed free access to the United States market. The availability and —in the absence of political uncertainty and exchange rate variations— the stability of the American market makes it possible for Puerto Rico to concentrate on those industries in which she possesses cost advantages.[30] On the other hand, tariffs and other artificial obstacles to trade restrict Chile's possibilities to develop export-oriented industries and

[28] *Ibid.*, p. 353.
[29] The reader will note that our conclusions apply to a much less degree to the United States where the large domestic market appeared as a powerful stimulus.
[30] See Werner Baer, "Puerto Rico: An Evaluation of a Successful Development Program", *Quarterly Journal of Economics*, November, 1959, pp. 645-71.

the expansion of manufacturing industries is also limited by the smallness of the domestic market.

In general, underdeveloped countries face the choice between the parallel development of a number of industries and the concentrated growth of a few branches of manufacturing. Both these methods have certain advantages and disadvantages. To begin with, the first method would provide external economies for the industries in question through their interrelationships in production and their interdependence via increased incomes. By reason of the observed interdependence in production, the manufacturing of any commodity becomes more profitable the greater is the availability of the necessary inputs, complementary goods, and outlets. In the expression of Professor Scitovsky, "it is generally desirable and profitable to expand simultaneously, and in the proportions determined by technological production coefficients, the production and productive capacity of all goods whose relation to each other is that of factor to product or common factor to the same product".[31] Similarly, consumer demand for the products of any industry depends on incomes generated through the expansion of other industries.

Potential external economies that find their origin in the interdependence of industries in production and consumption would speak for the simultaneous expansion of all interrelated industries. In most underdeveloped countries, however, various limitations interfere with the parallel development of a number of industries. These limitations include the availability of productive factors (e. g., skilled labor), the rate of investment, and the size of the market. On the supply side, the quantities of factors of production available and the

[31] "Growth — Balanced or Unbalanced?", in *The Allocation of Economic Resources*, Essays in Honor of B. F. Haley, Stanford: Stanford University Press, 1959, p. 211.

146

feasible amount of new investment, on the demand side, the insufficiency of the existing market outlets restrict simultaneous advances on all fronts. Given these limitations, production units of efficient size will not be profitable and thus potential economies of scale will be foregone.

Supply limitations would permit the exploitation of economies of scale if the available resources were used for developing a limited number of industries. Concentrated growth may also be more conducive to technological progress since a fast rate of expansion gives scope to the introduction of new technological methods. This proposition finds support in the evidence supplied on the interrelationship of the rate of increase of output and the growth of productivity. Concentrated growth will meet with important barriers on the demand side, however. Since domestic demand is unlikely to follow the lopsided production pattern, discrepancies will be created between the structure of demand and supply. The time-honored method of removing this discrepancy is foreign trade. Yet, under present-day conditions, the expansion of exports in new lines of production faces difficulties by reason of the obstacles and uncertainties in foreign trade. In addition, the newly developed industries are unlikely to attain cost advantages since they will not enjoy external economies that would result from the development of related industries. In other words, the comparative advantage of any given industry will depend on inter-industry interrelationships. As a result, nations that concentrate their development in a limited number of industries often face the unhappy choice between installing plants of less than optimum capacity and building ahead of demand. The second alternative has been chosen in several Latin American countries where a large number of firms

147

operate with excess capacity, especially in Argentina and Mexico, but also in Brazil.[32]

The arguments presented here should suffice to demonstrate the difficulties underdeveloped countries face in balanced and in unbalanced growth.[33] Many of these obstacles can be removed if the market is enlarged through integration. In the latter case, the external economies associated with the simultaneous development of interrelated industries can be appropriated, and the advantages of concentrated growth can also be exploited. The possibility of reaping external economies through the interdependence of industries in production and in consumption appears, then, as a powerful argument for economic integration.[34] Integration is not a panacea for curing all economic ills, however, and its beneficial effects will follow only if sociological, psychological, and political obstacles to development can be surmounted. Finally, the position taken in this paper should not be interpreted as a plea for less trade. Besides increased trade relations within the integrated area, increasing productivity should also contribute to the competitiveness of export industries as well as to a rising de-

[32] Examples are machine-tools, household electric appliances, electric motors, artificial fibers, rubber tires, bicycles, etc.

[33] We have concentrated our attention here on those aspects of the balanced-unbalanced growth controversy that are relevant to our topic. The reader can find valuable material on the broader issues of this problem in previously-cited writings of Nurkse, Lewis, and Hirschman, as well as in Paul Streeten, "Unbalanced Growth", Oxford Economic Papers, June, 1959, pp. 167-190, and Tibor Scitovsky, "Growth — Balanced or Unbalanced?", in The Allocation of Economic Resources, pp. 207-17, to which this exposition owes much.

[34] For similar conclusions, see W. Baer, op. cit., Quarterly Journal of Economics, pp. 66-67, 670; T. Scitovsky, op. cit., en The Allocation of Economic Resources, pp. 216-17;, and John Sheahan, "International Specialization and the Concept of Balanced Growth", Quarterly Journal of Economics, May, 1958, p. 197.

mand for imports from third countries as a consequence of increased incomes.

These conclusions can be applied to Latin America, for example. The fusion of national markets in this area is expected to make possible simultaneous advances in a number of fields as well as application of large-scale technological methods in individual industries. The enlargement of the market will also permit the development of new branches of manufacturing, especially in the field of metallurgy, metal manufacturing, and engineering. Both the emergence of new industries and the expansion of old ones can contribute to the utilization of hitherto unused or underutilized resources, particularly labor and mineral supplies, and can lead to induced technological improvements.[35] Non-market interactions are likely to be of importance, too, inasmuch as integration can result in the spreading of existing knowledge among particular industries of different countries, and the closer contact between competing national industries may increase the rate of technological change.

SPECIALIZATION IN A LARGE MARKET

So far we have discussed non-market interaction between industries and external economies operating through the market under the assumption that the structure of existing industries remains unchanged. However, an increase in the extent of the market also changes the structure of individual industries. Allyn Young first pointed out in his justly celebrated article the impact of an enlargement of the market on specialization.

[35] For an attempt to measure numerically the extent of external economies in the steel industry and metal manufacturing in Latin America under varying assumptions, see H. B. Chenery, "The Interdependence of Investment Decisions", in *The Allocation of Economic Resources*, pp. 82-120.

Young emphasized that the larger market makes it possible to segregate various functions of an industry into specialized undertakings that will then constitute new industries. This diversification process allows for the use of specialized machinery and leads to specialization in labor and management. Young notes that the scale of operations of the newly created industries "merely reflects the size of the market for final products of the industry or industries to whose operations their own are ancillary. And the principal advantage of large scale operation at this stage is that it again makes methods economical which would be uneconomical if their benefits could not be diffused over a large final product".[36]

Subsequently, Young's ideas were further developed by Professor Stigler. Stigler expounds that certain processes carried out by the firm are subject to increasing, and others to decreasing, returns. At a given time, these functions may be too small to support a specialized firm or firms. With an increase in output, processes subject to increasing returns will be taken up in the framework of a new firm (or firms) constituting a new industry (or industries). Stigler adds that the firms specializing in these activities cannot wield monopoly power since the demand for their products is elastic: the old firms will refuse to pay a price higher than the average cost of the process to them. With a further expansion of the market, the newly created industry becomes competitive and the splitting of processes continues.[37]

[36] "Increasing Returns and Economic Progress", *Economic Journal*, December, 1928, p. 539. Young illustrates his theory with the case of the printing trade, where the printers were originally producers of wood-pulp, paper, type metal, specialized tools and machines, etc., which functions have later become separate industries.

[37] G. J. Stigler, "The Division of Labor is Limited by the Extent of the Market", *Journal of Political Economy*, June, 1951,

More generally, the greater is the extent of the market, the larger will be the economies of specialization. A small market may permit the maintenance of one or even a few optimal plants producing certain machines or durable consumer goods, but a small country will not be able to produce various parts, components, accessories, and capital goods on an optimum scale, and will not sustain the optimum operation of certain subsidiary and ancillary activities. The importation of components, accessories, etc., is not a remedy, partly because in most cases the final products are not homogenous, partly because repair services and training facilities may not be accessible.

The interrelationship between the size of the market and specialization has been studied in respect to various industries. A favored example of the process of disintegration concomitant with increased output is that of the metal industry in the Birmingham area in Britain. There, plants have come to specialize vertically in certain processes and services such as foundry, casting, forging, tool-making, and repairs, and horizontally in the manufacture of needles and pins, safes and locks, domestic hollow-ware, electric heaters and cooking apparatus, batteries, electrical machinery, etc. The subdivision of processes also conferred advantages on the British textile industry over, e. g., German textile manufacturing where specialization was less developed.[38]

---

pp. 185-93. It can be added that there is no need for assuming that some processes exhibit intrinsically increasing, and others decreasing returns. The economies of specialization are connected rather with changes in technology, when the cost curves of different activities will shift downwards as the expansion of the market makes the application of hitherto not used technological methods possible. Processes that on a small scale exhibited increasing costs in the relevant range will then be operated at lower unit costs as output expands.

[38] Cf. R. Sargant Florence, *Investment, Location, and the*

151

The automobile industry is another frequently used example. Bain notes that inter-firm interchangeability of automobile parts between United States producers makes possible the exploitation of large scale economies in their production. This applies to the manufacture of such components as electrical and ignition systems, heaters, steering wheels, hydraulic brakes, bearings, oil pumps, transmissions, batteries, spark plugs, gauges, radiators, springs, etc.[39] These parts and accessories had been originally manufactured by the car producers, and have come to be produced by separate undertakings as the output of cars increased. The period after the Second World War has seen an increased degre of subcontracting and many small enterprises were formed to supply a certain producer with one or more components.

Considering the present level of economic development in Latin American countries, integration may bring considerable gains from specialization in this area. The United Nations Economic Commission for Latin America studied the possibilities of specialization in the pulp and paper industry and in cotton textiles.[40] Similar conclusions have been reached with regard to several branches of heavy industry, too.[41] Possibilities for specialization in various manufacturing industries can be illustrated by the example of Brazil, who possesses the largest national market in Latin America. In

Size of the Plant, Cambridge, At the University Press, 1948, pp. 54-7, and Sidney Chapman, Work and Wages, vol. I, p. 166.

[39] J. S. Bain, Barriers to New Competition, p. 247.

[40] Pulp and Paper Industry in Latin America, United Nations, New York, 1955, and Labor Productivity of the Cotton Textile Industry in Five Latin American Countries, United Nations, 1951. On Central America, see La Integración Económica de Centroamérica, Ch. VI.

[41] Cf., e. g., Plácido García Reynoso, "Probables efectos del Tratado de Montevideo en la industrialización de América Latina", El Trimestre Económico, April-June, 1960, pp. 193-202.

the latter country, an increased degree of specialization has been observed in recent years in metal manufacturing and engineering. In the production of electrical motors, electrical and gas ranges, sewing machines, metal furniture, for example, there has been a tendency to subcontract the foundry part of the production process and, to a lesser extent, also various operations, such as stamping, forging, thermal treatments, etc., to specialized firms. The Brazilian automobile industry provides another example. Prior to the introduction of automobile production in Brazil, a large number of automobile parts and components were manufactured for replacement in one or two plants. Presently, only one or two parts or components are produced in each plant, and these specialized plants are of smaller size than establishments that had a more diversified production pattern.[42]

It should be noted, however, that gains from specialization can be partly offset by transportation costs. This consideration has relevance for the Latin American Free Trade Association where economic distances between Mexico and Argentina, or between Brazil and Chile, will interfere with intra-industry specialization between these countries. Specialization, then, can contribute to agglomerative tendencies, but these lie outside of our chosen subject matter and will not be discussed here.

[42] For information concerning the Brazilian experience, I am indebted to Nuno Fidelino de Figueiredo, Research Director of the U. N. Economic Commission for Latin America.

CONTENTS

CHAPTER I

INTEGRATION OF DEVELOPING COUNTRIES AND CUSTOMS UNION THEORY

CHAPTER II

EXPORTS AND ECONOMIC GROWTH

ALTERNATIVE STRATEGIES FOR
ECONOMIC GROWTH

LARGE SCALE ECONOMIES
AND INTEGRATION

157

Printed and made in Mexico by
Gráfica Panamericana, S. de R.
L., 911 Parroquia St., Mexico
12, D. F. Copies: 2 000. February 27, 1965.

Nº 01696

PB-0011665
532-22

PB-001665
532-22

DATE DUE

12. 16. '82	
APR 2 9 '92	
FEB 1 2 1999	
APR 1 4 1999	

BRODART, INC   Cat. No. 23-221

3 5209 00416 4410